water...

HOW IT TORE A REGION APART and BROUGHT IT BACK TOGETHER AGAIN
THE STORY of CASCADE WATER ALLIANCE

WRITTEN BY
ELAINE KRAFT

CASCADE WATER ALLIANCE
BELLEVUE, WA

Water... How it Tore a Region Apart and Brought it Back Together Again The Story of Cascade Water Alliance. Copyright © 2016 by Cascade Water Alliance, Bellevue, WA. All rights reserved. Printed in the United States. No part of this book may be used or reproduced in any manner whatsoever without written permission from Cascade Water Alliance except in the case of brief quotations. For information address Cascade Water Alliance, 520 112th Avenue NE, Suite 400, Bellevue, WA 98004.

Produced by Cascade Water Alliance
Printed by A&A Printing, Seattle, WA
Design: Sarah Conradt-Kroehler

ISBN: 978-0-692-65285-5

FIRST EDITION

DEDICATION

Cascade Water Alliance would not have been created, nor this history written, without the more than three decades of committed and dedicated work of Lloyd Warren. This project began under his auspices as Utilities Manager at the City of Bellevue beginning in 1985 and continues to this day. In his ongoing service to Cascade and the region, he has served as a board member and as past chair. This book is dedicated to him, whose vision, heart and soul made Cascade a reality.

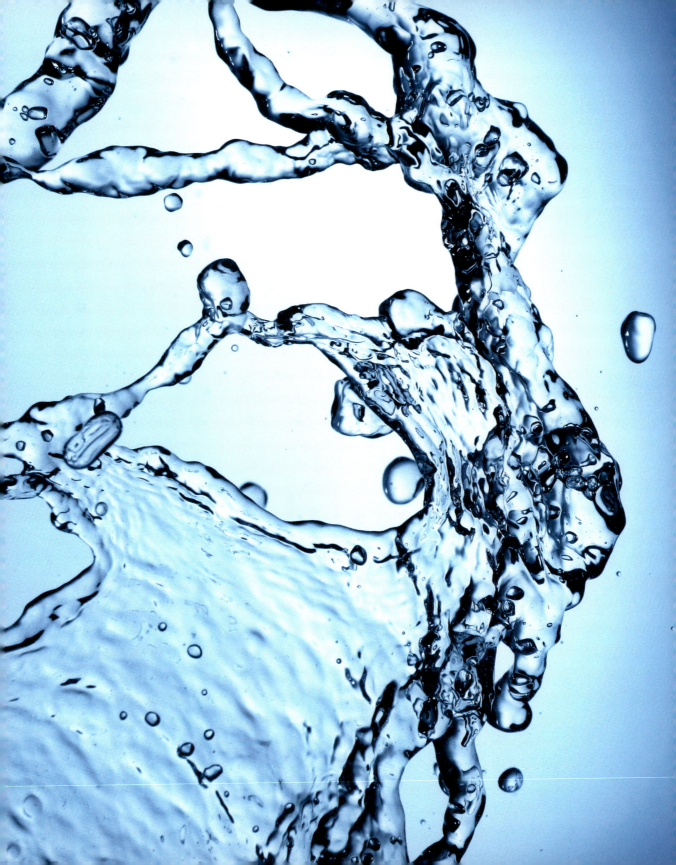

"We all need water. Together we can mitigate the challenges that may face us, and we are stronger together than apart. That was always our vision."

MARY ALYCE BURLEIGH

Cascade Board Member,
City of Kirkland

PROLOGUE
PLANNING FOR TOMORROW

News Advisory—2016: The Central Puget Sound Water Supply Forum, comprised of Seattle Public Utilities, Tacoma Water, the City of Everett, Cascade Water Alliance and other water providers in the region, will today release findings and recommendations on the emergency preparedness the region must take to deal with the impacts of earthquakes, climate change, drought and water quality on water supply. The report and recommendations are the result of two years of coordinated, inclusive, integrated scientific study aimed at ensuring the region's utilities will be prepared to handle emergencies together in the future.

Water... then and now

It doesn't stop at the border of each jurisdiction through which it meanders. It doesn't plan for economic development or growth or the future needs of a region that relies on water.

But others do. Like visionary leaders throughout that region. Like those who watch and protect natural resources, and, eventually even the residents in the region do.

This is a story of how water divided a community, and how leadership and cooperation brought it together again.

It's also a story about today. How more than 30 years after the 'water wars' many of the same regional leaders who fought over water have come together to ensure its future. Their goal is to get the region ready to help each other be prepared should anything happen to that precious resource—water. And they want to make sure that all of those who take it for granted today will be just as confident for generations that when they turn on the tap in their homes and businesses years from now, water will always flow.

It's a story told by those who were there, then and now.

ACKNOWLEDGMENTS

Cascade Water Alliance brings together all the elements of what is good about government—regionalism, forward thinking, dedication and inclusiveness—and it breaks down all the traditional challenges facing government—bureaucracy, glacial pace and territorialism.

The result has been a new type of organization. Cascade Water Alliance crosses boundaries and tackles what needs to be addressed while planning for the future. It is a collection of similar minded entities, elected leaders and the communities each represents combining to provide essential public services that can be done better together than separately. It is also a lean, nimble, vision-driven coalition working together to provide essential public services in an environmentally and economically sound manner. Reaping the benefits are the residents of the central Puget Sound region.

Cascade has its roots in its desire for a voice and a vote. Water issues created controversy and divided a region. Yet its efforts have helped bring the region together again. It's a story of the people who care about the people they serve and how they can make tomorrow better.

This history would not be a reality without the help and leadership of Jon Ault, Paula Anderson, Alison Bennett, Bonney Lake Historical Society, Mike Brent, Pat Brodin, Shawn Bunney, Mary Alyce Burleigh, Fred Butler, Walt Canter, Ken Castile, Ed Cebron, Tim Ceis, John Clark, Chuck Clarke, Don Davidson, Grant Degginger, Chandler Felt, Diana Gale, Gene Galloway, Joel Gordon, Adam Gravely, Jim Haggerton, Scott Hardin, Rhonda Hilyer, Ray Hoffman, Rosemarie Ives, Fred Jarrett, Bob King, Sarah Langton, Terry Lukens, Sheldon Lynne, Doreen Marchione, John Marchione, Ralph Mason, Gwenn Maxfield, Joe Mickelson, Jim Miller, Linda Moreno, Chuck Mosher, Ed Oberg, Bob Pancoast, Chris Paulucci, T.C. Richmond, Dan Roach, Pam Roach, Bob Roegner, Charles Romeo, Norman B. Rice, Jan Shabro, Ed Shield, Jon Shimada, Kirk Shuler, Ron Sims, Ron Speer, Betty Spieth-Croll, Hugh Spitzer, John Stokes, Penny Sweet, Scott Thomasson, Lloyd Warren, Bob Wilderman and countless others.

During completion of this history, Lake Tapps leader Leon Stucki passed away, leaving a void in that community as well as with Cascade. He was a true champion of the lake and it was a pleasure and honor to be able to work with him on its future.

Special thanks to Michael Gagliardo, the longest serving Cascade staff member who led Cascade in its infancy and helped keep it going through some tough times. He made this history a reality, and it is with him that the institutional knowledge of Cascade resides.

Additional thanks to two outstanding community relationship builders, Betty Spieth-Croll and Sarah Langton, who helped with all outreach, ensuring the resulting successes become reality.

And thanks to Mavis Lamb, who edited our collective recollection into a wonderful story and designer Sarah Conradt-Kroehler who brought it to life.

A story is only valuable if it is shared and others can learn from it. Thank you all for letting me be a part of Cascade, and letting me lend my skills and passion for government, media, community outreach and relationship building to this effort.

CONTENTS

1	FROM SEATTLE EASTWARD	2
2	GETTING TO YES	14
3	CASCADE WATER ALLIANCE	26
4	DIVINING FOR WATER	40
5	CASCADE'S TODDLER YEARS	58
6	CASCADE'S NEW NEIGHBORS – THE TRIBES	68
7	CASCADE'S NEW NEIGHBORS – THE HOMEOWNERS	78
8	CASCADE'S NEW NEIGHBORS – THE FOUR CITIES	96

9	PUTTING ALL THE PIECES TOGETHER	104
10	CELEBRATING NEW BEGINNINGS	110
11	COALITION BUILDING AND LEGISLATIVE FIXES	124
12	RESCUING THE RESERVOIR WATER FOR THE FUTURE	146
13	ADOLESCENCE, AND HEADING TOWARD ADULTHOOD	162
APPENDIX A – Cascade Key Documents		178
APPENDIX B – Cascade Chronology		180
APPENDIX C – Cascade Board Members		182

1.
FROM SEATTLE EASTWARD

The 1960s was an amazing time for Seattle. The gem of the Pacific Northwest was a glistening portal to the east, west, north and south. The city boomed with business and buzzed with social, cultural and civic pride.

The 1962 World's Fair—Century 21—ushered in a peek at the future with the Space Needle shooting skyward and the gleaming monorail cutting its way from the sprawling Seattle Center through downtown to Westlake. Riders departed just steps away from I. Magnin, Nordstrom (still to be combined with its neighbor Best Apparel) and Marshall Field's Frederick & Nelson, where white-gloved elevator operators guided shoppers to their destination.

Neighborhoods thrived, creating a variety of unique communities throughout the city. Seattle's 557,000 residents spent fall Saturdays cheering at Husky Stadium. The Seattle Rainiers played baseball in Sick's Seattle Stadium, with home plate looking directly at Mount Rainier. Residents celebrated Seafair on the first Sunday in August with mighty hydroplanes like Bardahl, Hawaii Kai and Slo Mo roaring around Lake Washington. Families were entertained by gorillas Bobo and Fifi, the Woodland Park Zoo's star attractions. Diners frequented fine restaurants like Rosellini's 410, Canlis and Franco's Hidden Harbor. And major medical facilities proliferated on First Hill, or "Pill Hill." The stately Smith Tower, then the tallest building in the west at 462 feet, stood as a magnificent beacon over all this optimism. The newly constructed Interstate 5 made access throughout the city easy and convenient.

Yet in the midst of this idyllic city, as in communities around the country, life was about to change.

Opposite: (clockwise from top left) Space Needle during Seattle's World's Fair; Monorail; City Light float, Seafair; Downtown skyline and Interstate 5; Sick's Seattle Stadium; Smith Tower
(All photos courtesy Seattle Municipal Archives Collection)

VIEW FROM A BRIDGE

While most Seattleites focused on their city and the gorgeous sunsets over Puget Sound, the sun was rising every day over an ever growing Eastside. As far back as 1921, some forward thinkers, including engineer Homer Hadley, saw the need for a bridge to connect Seattle area goods and products with the rest of the country. Almost 20 years later, prior to World War II, that need continued to grow. In 1939, the completion of construction of a floating bridge across Lake Washington started at a cost of about $9 million.

While the bridge eased the connection between Seattle and the east, it also paved the way for tremendous growth in several new suburban "bedroom" communities including Bellevue, Mercer Island and Kirkland, and, at a slower rate, communities like Redmond and Issaquah. The bridge, and the foresight of one family, launched Bellevue on its way to becoming the hub of the Eastside. Just four years after the bridge was completed Miller Freeman and his son, Kemper, Sr., began buying property. By 1946, they opened the Bel-Vue Theater. The Crabapple Restaurant and the Kandy Kane Motel followed. By year's end, the Freeman family added a feather in its cap with a new phenomenon in

Bellevue Way from Main, 1928

Bellevue—the first Eastside shopping center. Frederick & Nelson and JC Penney were early anchor stores, and Newberry's lunch counter did a thriving business. With plenty of land for building and parking, several new businesses sprouted in what had been strawberry fields. The City of Bellevue incorporated in 1953, and became the heart of the Eastside just as the Freemans had imagined.

There was so much growth that a second floating bridge was built. The Evergreen Point Floating Bridge (SR 520) opened in 1963, and brought even more access to north Bellevue and Kirkland, and with access came additional new residents to the Eastside. Workers could easily commute to their jobs in downtown Seattle, still the primary employment area, and be back in their "country" communities for dinner.

Amenities soon followed, such as medical facilities, parks and outstanding schools. Neighborhoods established community swimming pools and tennis courts, local baseball fields, and later, soccer fields. In addition to the new shopping center, the John Danz Theater, Belle Lanes bowling alley and two drive-in theaters opened on the Eastside, all spelling an easy, comfortable quality suburban life. With Seattle fairly developed, those families who wanted a new, affordable home with a large yard and maybe some land, looked to the very appealing Eastside communities.

Growth accelerated when a new north-south "truck route," Interstate 405, cut through the Eastside suburbs connecting to I-5 but bypassing Seattle. Farms throughout the region began to disappear, giving way to new planned communities and light industrial areas. Suburbanites and growth were here to stay.

By 1970, Seattle's population had dropped to 531,000, down 46,000 people. Seattleites who could afford "the better life" left for the suburbs, and safer, cleaner neighborhoods across the bridges. Economic downturn and resulting job loss combined to drive families away. Billboards along I-5, following the Boeing bust in which residents lost their jobs, asked the last person leaving Seattle to turn out the lights.

In 1980, Seattle's population had further dropped to 493,000, while Bellevue's was on a steady climb to almost 80,000. Witnessing the explosive growth in their community, Bellevue civic leaders and elected officials had their eyes on the future. They became convinced that Bellevue should be the master of its own destiny and that they could and should shape that future.

PLANNING AHEAD

Communities cannot grow without planning, and they can't plan for future growth without water to support that growth. At that time, three small water districts served the Bellevue area, but local leaders knew the importance of eventually controlling the water their city needed for the future. The Seattle Water Department historically provided water not only to its own residents since its inception in 1854, but also to contiguous communities like Ballard, West Seattle, Renton, the Rainier Valley, Alderwood and growing communities just outside and around its borders. But what about Bellevue and the rest of the Eastside?

As early as June 1935, Seattle discussed building a pipeline to the east side of Lake Washington to serve Eastside residents. W. C. Morse, Superintendent of Water, found that financial grants and loans were available to pay for such work. He said the Eastside pipeline was a very real issue for the "overlake communities," but added that the Eastside issue was different from serving the communities adjacent to the city which would likely eventually be incorporated into the city, and should be treated differently from the start. Morse is said to have believed that the Eastside could never be served by an extension of the existing distribution system and should have an entirely separate system.

According to the official Seattle Water Department history by Mary Williams, "There should be no retailing of water by the city in the area, but that future service would be rendered only by wholesaling to water districts which in turn would provide individual distribution systems for retailing the water bought from the city."

Williams' history states that Seattle did not recognize "at this time any responsibility to serve this district but was willing to do so as soon as a water district (Eastside) was formed that could officially speak for

Enatai neighborhood sign, 1950

Meydenbauer Bay, Bellevue in the background, 1964

the entire area and enter into binding contracts that would protect the interests of the city as well as their own."

By February 1939 boundaries for a proposed Eastside water service plan were established by King County Commissioners and an election was set to ratify it. A vote was set for those residents within the proposed service area on April 22, 1939. Since Mercer Island, Redmond, Hunts Point, Yarrow Point, Kirkland, Bothell and Weowna Beach (Bellevue) already had active water utility systems they were excluded from the plan. But the vote lost 899-821.

By 1950, Seattle had conducted studies of future water needs that led to the Seattle City Council approving development of the south fork of the Tolt River as a secondary source of municipal water supply in 1952. Seattle took steps to secure both a large municipal water right for reservoirs on the Tolt River and permits to use the water. The city began

Left: Intersection of Bel-Red Road and 140th Avenue NE, 1963; Right: Bellevue Square, 1967

developing the Tolt water supply, which came on line around 1960 for the Seattle system and its customers. This was primarily for use by the growing Eastside, even though many communities used independent supplies from other water districts like Rose Hill. The problem was that these supplies would not have sufficient quantities to serve ever growing needs, so additional sources would be needed.

The Tolt water supply was a major break from the past, as it officially signaled that Seattle was becoming a regional water supplier. Prior to that, Seattle had only provided water from its Cedar River source to those on the actual transmission line—Renton and adjacent cities.

The construction of a pipeline connected the Cedar to the Tolt River system. The system ran from east of Woodinville, down 140th Avenue in Bellevue, down to Renton in the south about two miles east of the Interstate 405 corridor and then west to Mercer Island. It was a prelude to Seattle providing water to the Eastside.

The Tolt water supply worked, but during the '60s and '70s supply concerns surfaced because the "growth of the Eastside was so exponential," explained Jim Miller, Superintendent of Everett Water, who was then an engineer with the City of Seattle. He added that since contracts between Seattle and Eastside cities were set to expire in 1982, discussions about the future of water supply were ongoing.

In one such discussion during the early 1970s, Miller was charged with reviewing the potential for Bellevue using water from Lake Hancock and Lake Callahan on the North Fork of the Snoqualmie River for the city's future growth. "It didn't look good," he recalls.

In another discussion, because there had been extensive flooding on the Snoqualmie River, Miller said Seattle was pushed to control it. A site was selected on the middle fork to build a dam, but it faced extensive opposition from the environmental community. A mediator gathered the US Army Corps of Engineers, Snoqualmie Valley officials and environmental interests. A compromise was reached to build a smaller dam, not on the middle fork, but on the north fork of the Snoqualmie River.

By the end of the decade, Seattle was supplying drinking water to 32 wholesale customers including Bellevue, other cities and water districts on the Eastside. Seattle faced the very real threat of customers leaving or developing sources on their own, so the city offered contracts guaranteeing customers' long-term water supply. Having already annexed the three former water districts that had served its residents, Bellevue now had a water utility as part of its city government. However, Bellevue and others wanted greater assurances on financial issues and rates from Seattle.

Miller, the lead negotiator for Seattle with all the water districts, recalls that the process dragged on and on. Many cities and districts were not happy with the proposed contracts, yet were without other water sources. They felt they had no alternative but to sign. In 1982, despite the unhappiness of cities and districts, 27 entered into 30-year contracts with Seattle locking up water supply through 2012.

NO VOICE AND NO VOTE

Beyond being unhappy with their new contracts in 1982, Bellevue and other Eastside cities felt penalized for having growing communities. Pricing for Seattle's existing retail customers (its residents and businesses) was 23 cents per hundred cubic feet (CCF). But there was an overarching

> "We didn't have an ownership interest in the system and the Seattle City Council controlled water. The Eastside paid the expense to expand the Seattle system and yet didn't have a say in how it was done."

policy that Eastside and other wholesale customers pay for the cost to service any new growth. Seattle bore the responsibility to obtain additional water to serve these new wholesale customers, but believed the new customers should have to pay for it. That translated into a rate that was double the charge Seattle customers paid. Wholesale customers could take what they were currently using, but for any water over that amount they had to pay the new water surcharge. This meant only those who were growing were paying more of the new water charge.

Dr. Don Davidson, a Bellevue dentist, was then serving as president of the Bellevue Chamber of Commerce and had done a considerable amount of work on water supply issues to help Bellevue grow. He reflected on those rates, saying "We didn't have an ownership interest in the system and the Seattle City Council controlled water. The Eastside paid the expense to expand the Seattle system and yet didn't have a say in how it was done."

Davidson explains that Eastsiders objected to being what they called "renters." Seattle kept its rates low to its own residents, while the Eastsiders paid a new rate created just for them.

Following the signing of the 1982 contracts, the push was on to find other water sources. Davidson, who went on to serve Bellevue as a City Council member and Mayor on and off until 2013, created the "Eastside Venture" to explore building a dam on the north fork of the Snoqualmie River for a source of drinking water for Bellevue and the Eastside. The Eastside Venture was a collection of those purveyors interested in joining with Bellevue to leave the Seattle system. Other purveyors were involved to some extent in the project to build a dam on the north fork, with both financial assistance

Longtime activist and Bellevue elected official Dr. Don Davidson

and political support. The group became focused on examining how to approach Seattle to change the current arrangements. While a dam might be economically and environmentally feasible, group members knew political support was fractured.

When Davidson and others went to the Washington State Legislature to get approval for a new dam, they faced opposition from Puget Sound Energy (PSE) and the City of Seattle, but their measure passed. The Federal Energy Regulatory Commission (FERC) referred the issue back to the local region, where it went no further. "We were growing. We needed water. We wanted a voice and a vote and to control our own destiny," Davidson said. After that, the Eastside Venture floundered for lack of support and rising costs of studies.

In 1985, Lloyd Warren, a 10 year veteran at the City of Bellevue, became its new Utilities Manager. His first task on the new job—extricate Bellevue from its efforts to get water from north fork of the Snoqualmie River by finally shutting down the Eastside Venture, and, at the same time, find a way for Bellevue to have some ownership in its water resources. This, he said, was the start of the effort to organize regionally.

"When the Bellevue City Council terminated its pursuit of an independent water supply project, it supported a regional water supply governance solution," Warren said.

Don Wright, a consultant with the City of Auburn and a Commissioner of the Woodinville Water District at this time, agreed. The main issue was that the Seattle Water Department did not give purveyors any input into the operation of the water system or decisions about future supply. Anger was percolating. A request was made to have independent reviews performed on the Seattle rate studies, specifically collective costs and the costs to the purveyors, but Seattle refused.

The State Department of Health was pushing for the completion of Coordinated Water System Plans. An administrator was needed to monitor and oversee the plan, so the East King County Regional Water Association (EKCRWA) was created to determine critical issues and to be the administrative agency for the plan. Don Wright was president of the EKCRWA and Bellevue's Lloyd Warren its staff. A South King County Regional Water Association (SKCRWA) was also established.

"We were growing. We needed water. We wanted a voice and a vote and to control our own destiny."

Technically, the EKCRWA didn't have any input into any plan. With the Eastside Venture folded, the EKCWRA undertook planning for a coordinated water system plan. And, while Bellevue still wanted a voice and vote in future water supply issues, participants were split on what exactly to do next.

Bob Pancoast, a hydro-geologist consultant who did groundwater studies for Eastside utilities and water districts, became the director of EKCRWA. All he knew was that the Seattle contracts had been difficult. While it may have seemed Seattle itself was onerous and that it was 'our way or the highway," he added in hindsight that a lot of the next steps were not as much vision, but more born out of distrust of Seattle and each side wanting to do things its own way.

Purveyors were still in discussions with Seattle regarding a planning process for water supply through 1996. They were asking if control could be different and if arrangements could be changed.

Don Wright added, "Had Seattle said yes to a real partnership between itself and the water providers that had contracts with them at the time, we might have had the agreements we were looking for and no acrimony."

The discussions continued to get more and more heated over the next few years. Animosity boiled just under the surface. There was anger, but also a determination to look out for one's own destiny. A major clash seemed unavoidable.

As a result, Seattle Mayor Norm Rice and Bellevue Mayor Terry Lukens got involved in the water discussions in early 1990. Mayor Rice, long recognized for his commitment to regional solutions, agreed to begin talks. Rice had been on the Seattle City Council since 1978. He is widely credited with revitalizing downtown Seattle during his tenure, and was respected by leaders in the suburbs for being inclusive and regional in his thinking and approach.

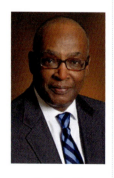

Seattle Mayor Norm Rice

Mayor Rice, who well understood the importance of the issue said, "I quickly saw it was setting up to be Seattle versus the region. That wouldn't work. I knew we had to broker a discussion. Ultimately, we all have to think regionally to get things done. Water is the greatest commodity we have, and we need to manage it well." He added that, "It's not just Seattle's water, it's all of our water. We need to give everyone a voice and a vote in decisions about our water. It's the only way to play."

With the ultimate respect for Terry Lukens, Rice believed that if they could get together, they could make something happen.

Bellevue Mayor
Terry Lukens

Lukens explained, "Norm was open to regional ideas, forming coalitions. He was open to discussions. We met several times and then met with stakeholders, suburban cities, water districts and Seattle. We determined principles. It was important groundwork if we were to move forward. There was a lot of tension between Seattle, Bellevue and the districts (who didn't trust either of us). Without Mayor Rice we could not have gotten this done. He got us to solutions."

Rice and Lukens pulled together a group and tasked it with creating a new regional water entity.

Called the Tri-Caucus effort, with Seattle, the Suburban Cities Association and the water districts (King County Water Alliance) its purpose was to frame a three party discussion to come to agreements on water supply in the region.

Today, Rice acknowledges there were bumps on the road. He got resistance from his Seattle Water Department and others in the city who thought "we were jeopardizing our watershed and giving away our water. I tried to have them think more regionally not just with water but with each issue," said Rice. "In the end, we were able to get it off the ground and get an important process started."

2.
GETTING TO YES

As the Tri-Caucus meetings began in 1991, participants came to the table with mixed emotions. Water purveyors throughout the region came to discuss their vital water supply, and while some were concerned about control and fairness, everyone wanted to have a say in how decisions would be made.

Former elected officials, Fred Jarrett, Mercer Island, Doreen Marchione, Redmond and Bob Roegner, Auburn with the author

Former leaders like Redmond's Mayor Doreen Marchione, Mercer Island Councilmember Fred Jarrett and Auburn Mayor Bob Roegner were supportive of a regional solution and favored the Municipality of Metropolitan King County (Metro) model for decision making. They felt its structure allowed every city in the region to have an elected official with an equal vote regardless of the number of people each jurisdiction represented. They would all have a voice and a vote, which so many at the table had desired for years. This approach showed them that when everyone participated, the process really worked. Fred Jarrett credits great stakeholders representing all constituencies in the region—and says that they listened to each other. "That's how you fashion better decisions," he said. "Being bound not by party or politics, but by the needs of the region, and with elected officials willing to act."

Hugh Spitzer, long-time Seattle lawyer and constitutional law professor, agreed. Spitzer, who is credited with creative solutions to municipal government operations, said, "Seattle tried to use an approach similar to the Metro model for the water talks. Mayor Norm Rice and Councilmembers Martha Choe and Jim Street were very open to regional perspectives. They were willing to consider making water a regional authority."

THE HAND THAT WAS DEALT

Still, Seattle held all the cards…and the water. Some contend Seattle was so protective of its water utility that they feared the city might not be an active participant. So stakeholders came to the table with optimism, suspicion, excitement, confusion, and a bit of bad blood. With this backdrop, the official regional Tri-Caucus discussions got underway.

The group was structured as a voluntary, informal exchange among elected officials. Its charge was to have a dialogue about water supply services for the region. Topics of discussion included decision making, cost sharing, reliability of supply, system ownership, financial burden and risk, as well as environmental and conservation policy.

Even though existing contracts were in place until 2012, the future was pressing. Water supply planning and implementation takes years. With the enormous growth of the metropolitan areas since 1982, most cities had gradually exceeded or discontinued the use of local sources, and instead requested water from Seattle's larger system.

As a result, the Seattle system faced challenges that were deemed beyond the capacities of both the present water supply and the existing governance structure: regional growth and the need for more water outside the area currently supplied by Seattle; urban development; federal and state drinking water quality regulations; water resource policies requiring more efficient, environmentally sensitive and better coordinated use of water; and growth management efforts were all challenges that needed to be addressed.

There were also important differences among faster versus slower growth jurisdictions; non-Seattle jurisdictions, those with their own water sources and those without; general purpose governments and special purpose districts; those with contracts for service from Seattle and those who wanted contracts. All these issues demanded a closely integrated water supply and water resource planning. But the priority was to determine how decisions would be made. At issue was whether there was sufficient interest and political will to initiate such a regional partnership, and whether it was worth breaking up the existing system. The initial

> "We are the elders of the region. If we can't figure out a way to get water issues sorted out instead of going to court, then 10 years from now other leaders will be sitting here still trying to figure this out. It's up to us."

response was yes, and in January 1991, a report was issued outlining these questions for the Tri-Caucus group.

TAKING DESTINY INTO THEIR OWN HANDS

Over the next several months, the Tri-Caucus group officially began its work. By the fall of 1992, the group entered into facilitated negotiations to identify a governance arrangement which would develop new water supplies.

Rhonda Hilyer, a well-known and respected facilitator in the region, was hired to bring some kind of consensus—if not solutions.

Representatives included participants from the East King County Regional Water Associations (EKRWA), Suburban Cities Association members (now Sound Cities Association) (SCA), South King County Water Resources Area (SKCRWA) and Seattle.

With a room full of unique individuals, competing interests and potential conflicts, Hilyer started by helping them identify their own and others' learning and working style. This exercise helped each 'player' get to know one another, build respect and demonstrate how to work together more effectively to garner real results. The group met regularly, usually at the Mercer Island Community Center—a location Hilyer says was neutral "much like Switzerland."

Mayor Rice addressed the initial gathering and implored others, saying "We are the elders of the region. If we can't figure out a way to get water issues sorted out instead of going to court, then 10 years from now other leaders will be sitting here still trying to figure this out. It's up to us."

While the discussions focused on future water governance options, it remained clear that Seattle alone had water. But what about the others at the table? Could they create something else for themselves? Could a new Metro-like entity be created? Should a new water entity be created? Should Seattle sell the new group its assets?

One participant, Scott Thomasson, the Utility Engineering Manager in the City of Redmond, acknowledged purveyors had to plan for their own water needs. Committees spent months looking at organizational structures, financial obligations and the building blocks of a potential new entity. Participants were charged with creating agreements in principle and policy directives that set the stage for a possible new water group. Another group continued to negotiate with Seattle for water supply. Seattle agreed to sell a new entity the water it didn't need over the next 30 years.

Sheldon Lynne, Issaquah's Deputy Director of Public Works, was at the table. While Issaquah had groundwater supply, the city's rapid growth meant it needed additional water. No new water rights were being granted, so for Lynne the issue was about controlling one's destiny. While the Tri-Caucus and EKCRWA were headed in one direction that suited their needs, Issaquah, Bellevue, Kirkland and Redmond withdrew from the EKCRWA planning efforts because the Tri-Caucus effort was better suited to their future water needs.

But moving forward on their own didn't mean smooth sailing.

Lynne recalls it being "testy and contentious, even though everyone there knew they needed to get a deal. We worked hard to figure out the future of water in the region."

There was no shortage of anger and hostility, even yelling and screaming among the many independent water districts.

At one point, Chip Davidson, a Northshore Utility District Commissioner, came into the room and pulled a hand grenade out of his pocket. He put it on the table in front of him and said "someone has to blow things up if we're going to make any progress!"

With the tension finally broken, real change was about to take place.

MOVING AHEAD

The almost two year-long effort to organize regional water supply management resulted in the decision that an entirely new entity was needed to determine how best to negotiate and deal with Seattle. In a Resolution of Intent Regarding Regional Water Supply Governance, issued in December 1993, the purveyors resolved that the "vision for regional water governance calls for the creation of an entity to plan for and develop new water sources. The entity would develop and manage new water supply sources in conjunction with existing regional water supply sources, with an emphasis on region-wide efficiency of operation and coordination among participating municipalities and adjacent regional water supply systems. The Tri-Caucus participants recognize that development of a new water supply source would be a multi-year process requiring coordination of many issues, therefore, the Tri-Caucus vision is for regional water governance and system planning promotion of coordinated sales of excess water supplies among municipalities in the region and promotion of coordinated water quality, water conservation and water reuse programs. The Tri-Caucus participants hereby state their intent to continue working together in 1994 and thereafter to further refine and promote this vision."

Participants envisioned the new entity as a "special purpose" organization with separate legal status that would not duplicate existing operations. And, until the new entity could be formally established, it would operate via interlocal agreements.

During 1994, the Tri-Caucus group further developed the concept of this new entity in terms of its functions, responsibilities, membership and financing. It also established a water planning link with King County. When an intertie with Tacoma Water became a viable major new source, the Tri-Caucus governance discussions became more focused. The Tri-Caucus group agreed on a consensus vision and additional principles to guide the new entity. The progress made during 1994 resulted in a 1995 work plan for the Tri-Caucus efforts.

The work plan stated the new entity would be established to finance,

> The almost two year-long effort to organize regionally resulted in the decision that an entirely new entity was needed to determine how best to negotiate and deal with Seattle.

construct and own and/or manage new regional water supplies. It would be open to membership from all municipalities within the service area and would be operated in an integrated manner to maximize supply availability and minimize system costs. It would avoid creation of a new bureaucracy. Incentives would be added for early participation by any municipalities in the region that were engaged in water supply planning and distribution. The financial integrity of the participating members would be respected.

Twenty of the 27 entities signed the agreement in December 1994—representatives from the water districts, the cities and Seattle. Next steps included extensive work in subcommittees developing organization and financial foundations. These subcommittees met intensively and regularly throughout most of the next few months and reported back to the entire group for review and approval of significant progress. The initial milestone was a final agreement on principles by June 30, 1995, outlining the functions, organizational structure, members' rights and responsibilities and development of a model for conducting regional water supply planning.

Seattle Mayor Rice, Bellevue Mayor Lukens and Ron Ricker, representing the water districts, signed a framework agreement called the "Guiding Vision." The agreement outlined regional water decision making and called for the development of a new water entity.

PROGRESS, BUT….

The official new entity, to be known as the Interim Water Group (IWG) was created to implement the work of the Tri-Caucus process. Gwenn Maxfield, then a Woodinville Water District commissioner, was named chair.

"...But we worked hard together," Maxfield recalls. "Emotions ran high. It was all very personal—like a family."

Gwenn Maxfield

The IWG's primary goal was to create a regional entity for future water operations, secure contracts with Seattle, and establish an organization and governance structure for the development of a regional water supplier as members would need water.

In 1995, the Financial Consulting Solutions Group (FCSG) was hired by IWG to help create a regional water authority, define governance and financial structure, create an interlocal agreement and develop water supply contracts with Seattle with a declining "wedge" block of water until the entity could get its own water.

Ed Cebron, then a principal of FCSG, reported the IWG needed to develop several products to implement the vision. These included:

- An institutional and financial arrangement to provide the power to plan, develop, own and operate regional water infrastructure;
- A financial structure to allocate costs and financial exposure in proportion to the benefits or services provided, while stable enough to support central bargaining;

- A wholesale supply contract with Seattle to transfer and revise rights and duties from individual purveyors to the new regional agency. The new entity would assume responsibility for contractual rights related to the Tacoma Second Supply Project; and
- An institutional and financial arrangement attractive enough to convince at least 75 percent of existing Seattle wholesale customers, by volume, to join.

Maxfield said members were galvanized, engaged and working as a tight, focused coalition.

The group had a lofty goal—to be its own master and no longer "have to kowtow to Seattle. Seattle saw a loss of revenue to them and opposed us having our own entity. But we worked hard together," Maxfield recalls. "Emotions ran high. It was all very personal—like a family."

Utilizing all the work done by Tri-Caucus and Interim Water Group efforts, the group forged ahead to meet its goal to have a recommended organizational structure ready for member approval by late 1997 or early 1998. The new entity would only become a reality if 75 percent of the current Seattle purveyors agreed to join in the next 18 months.

The negotiating meeting with the Seattle Water Department was held Nov. 12, 1996 at Kirkland City Hall. Notes indicate Diana Gale, then Seattle Water Superintendent, said the Interim Water Group should "know what they want as they approach Seattle." The Seattle City Council, she indicated, asked for scoping meetings to create a process together, rather than having Seattle doing it alone.

Gale published a special edition of the internal newsletter *"Seattle Water Leak!"* for purveyors with questions and answers about the process, calling it "an expressed intention of crafting an arrangement which did a better job of representing purveyor interest while still protecting Seattle's own interests. Seattle elected officials support the formation of a new entity and the principles agreement, provided 75 percent of individual purveyors, on the basis of water sales, support

Special Expanded Edition!

Seattle Water Leak!
INFORMATION UPDATE FOR PURVEYORS — SEPTEMBER 21, 1995

Questions & Answers Regarding Governance Process

Since Tri-Caucus members signed an Agreement of Principles on August 30, 1995, Seattle Water staff have been asked numerous questions regarding the governance process. Following are some of the more frequently asked questions and answers to them. I encourage you to call Ernie Dunston (684-5951) for a copy of the Agreement, as it is the basis for answers to many of your questions. I also encourage you to talk directly to the staff and elected officials of all three caucuses for their perspectives on these questions. — **DIANA GALE, Superintendent of Water**

1. *What is the Tri-Caucus?*
The Tri-Caucus is composed of representatives from three caucuses: 1) suburban cities; 2) water districts; and 3) Seattle, who have been working for the last three years to establish a new institutional framework for making regional water decisions and for developing new sources of water supply.

2. *How long have the governance talks been going on?*
Formal facilitated governance discussions started in 1992 with interim agreements reached in 1992, 1993 and 1994. The latest Agreement on Principles was signed this August (1995).

3. *When you speak of a "new regional water supply," what is the geographical area?*
Membership in the New Entity will be open to all jurisdictions within the King County urban service area, to all of Seattle's current contract purveyors, and to other jurisdictions at the discretion of the New Entity.

4. *Was the Agreement of Principles signed by district and city staff or elected officials?*
The agreement was signed by elected officials representing Seattle, suburban cities and water districts.

5. *Will the New Entity control the regional water supply?*
When the New Entity forms, it will be responsible for developing new sources to support the growth of its members. Baseline water will be provided to the New Entity under long-term contract with the City of Seattle. Seattle will convey its financial interest in Tacoma's Second Supply Project to the New Entity. Seattle will retain control over its Tolt, Cedar and Highline investments.

6. *Is Seattle trying to get out of its contracts with purveyors?*
No. Seattle entered into the governance process with an expressed intention of crafting an arrangement which did a better job of representing purveyor interests while still protecting its own interests. Purveyor interests, as expressed through their representation on the suburban cities and water district caucuses, have developed the concept of the New Entity as a vehicle for gaining greater control over their future water development plans. Seattle elected officials support the formation of the New Entity and the underlying Principles of Agreement, provided a 75% majority of individual purveyors (on the basis of water sales) support the New Entity and the agreement we have negotiated.

CONTINUED, page 2

Seattle Water newsletter, Sept. 21, 1995

the new entity and the agreement that had been negotiated. Seattle would honor contracts through 2012 to those who choose not to sign. After that, contracts could be renegotiated… Seattle recognizes its responsibility to be a regional partner in water supply."

A Bilateral Committee was established to negotiate the terms and conditions of an agreement between IWG and the City of Seattle. By January 1997, a draft of a proposed interlocal agreement was circulated, and the Bilateral Committee was focusing on what "firm yield" meant and cost/pricing methodologies.

"It was not a negotiation between two equal parties," Thomasson recalls. "Seattle said it had water and if the purveyors wanted it, these are the terms. There was considerable friction between Seattle and Bellevue. The potential and eventual formation of a new entity forced people to sit down, truly think about options and to make a conscious business decision. The reality of the IWG gave some utilities choices and forced others to analyze, make and live with their decisions."

Concerns for the future helped coalesce the group. Rosemarie Ives, Redmond mayor, felt the effort was critical. That city had groundwater but would need additional water for its future growth. "If we were going to grow as we had planned, we needed water to support it." Everyone knew the region would continue to grow and that they'd need water over time. Maxwell said, "It was incredible to be part of something so exciting. We had no idea how big it would become."

Seattle would continue to own, operate and control its existing regional supply systems, but provided notice that it would not continue the current water supply contracts after 2012. It would, however, sell the new entity any remaining water in excess of the demand of Seattle's direct service customers (firm yield.) Seattle would also be open to renegotiating contracts with any interested parties after the current contracts expired in 2012.

Cascade's first publication

"It was incredible to be part of something so exciting. We had no idea how big it would become."

Since negotiations often mean a change in rates, the rationale to purveyors was clear—if purveyors stayed with Seattle and Seattle had to build infrastructure to deliver that water, purveyors would have to pay for it. Purveyors asked why not just own it? Was it more expensive to create a new entity than simply continuing to buy water from Seattle? Perhaps yes, some felt, but others believed that having their own supply was worth it. To supporters, the choice was clearly creation of their own entity.

The Interim Water Group entity held a contest to name the new water group in March 1997. The IWG Update heralded the effort:

> "Name That Agency Contest
>
> Earn Fame! Win Food!
>
> Tired of the New Entity? Regional Think and other ad hoc labels?
>
> So are we.
>
> So, to further regional cooperation
>
> We are having a contest. Enter Early! Enter Often."

From left: Chuck Mosher, Lloyd Warren and Don Davidson, key Bellevue leaders

Bellevue Mayor Chuck Mosher offered up the name Cascade Water Alliance, which was selected.

Lloyd Warren says this was fitting. "Chuck's outstanding ability to build and foster relationships made him the perfect person to get the ball rolling. He helped set the tone, establish credibility and bring trust to the table." He further observed that from initial planning onward, Cascade always had (and would in continue to have in the future) the right person with the right skills in the right job at the right time to get success.

To join Cascade, members required:
- Seattle would use its present supplies to meet the needs of Seattle customers and would sell any excess supply to Cascade;
- Seattle would not have a need to develop new supply. Cascade would be responsible for developing new supplies to meet the growing needs of its members;
- Seattle wouldn't extend individual contracts beyond 2012 and would thus have only one wholesale agreement with Cascade;
- Members of Cascade would share equitably in the risks, costs and benefits in developing new supplies;
- Seattle would secure an interest in the Tacoma Second Supply Project on behalf of Cascade and at some point in the future would transfer equity and control of the project when the new entity bought out Seattle's interest.

The dream of so many was about to become a reality. Memos from Lloyd Warren to the Bellevue Environmental Services Commission and Bellevue City Council explained that the group was developing the necessary agreements to form a new entity for water supply. With the first new members' signatures on the interlocal agreement, Cascade Water Alliance would become a reality.

Everyone anticipated that the current Seattle purveyors would join. The clock was ticking. By Nov. 15, 1999, 75 percent of the contract purveyors, measured by water volume, would have to officially join the new entity before the agreement could become effective.

3.
CASCADE WATER ALLIANCE

It was official. On April 1, 1999, Cascade Water Alliance was created and the thoughts, plans, struggles and dreams of so many became a reality. The recruiting brochure touted the benefits Cascade provided, but also hinted at a sense of urgency…

> "Cascade Water Alliance offers independence from the current tenant status of the purveyors' agreement and provides supply insurance to member agencies by regionally sharing supplies, responsibilities, development efforts and risks. The formation of Cascade Water Alliance is underway, with membership available to current purveyors and urbanizing agencies. Water supply to regional members begins in 2000 and system buy-in fees are waived for agencies that join during the Cascade formation period. The time to join Cascade Water Alliance is now."

Primarily, Cascade was formed to provide water to its members with clear and decisive options to meet growing water demands. But it was also believed that when the current contracts with Seattle expired in 2012, there would be little freedom for purveyors to negotiate new contracts with the city.

Despite that, there seemed to be region-wide support for the new entity. Cascade's brochure went on to quote Margaret Pageler, Seattle City Councilmember, as saying, "The Cascade Water Alliance represents an opportunity for independence for suburban water suppliers. Seattle is pleased to help launch this new partnership." Moreover, then King

Cascade Water Alliance In 2011
Can You Count on Continued Water Supply?

Cascade Water Alliance

Join Cascade Water Alliance and play an active role in the development and management of reliable and known water supply for your customers.

Cascade Water Alliance delivers responsibility and leadership in a member-driven, regional approach to growing water demands and environmental issues.

More than seven years have been spent developing a long-term program benefiting member agencies and their customers.

Join for the Future of our Region

Cover of recruiting brochure, 1999

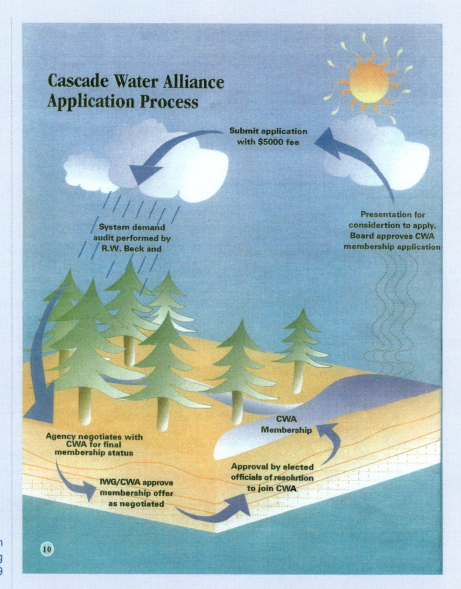

Page from recruiting brochure, 1999

County Executive Ron Sims and County Council Chair Louise Miller issued a statement that reiterated "King County supports and is interested in working with Cascade to coordinate, collaborate and partner on water resource issues." The county's support included the desire to build a regional coalition of water resource agencies for an integrated water resource strategy.

What Cascade was offering was something truly unique in the region—ownership and a voice for member agencies. More specifically, it was making a 50-year commitment to serve customers, maintain the quality and integrity of the environment and provide local water supply, and provide a regional approach to costs, supply, transmission and governance. It would be member owned and operated, with each member on equal standing with all other members which was a bit of a revolutionary approach in Puget Sound regional government. While each member would continue to prepare its own supply and system plans, Cascade would take responsibility for water supply.

Originally drafted by the Interim Water Group, Cascade had an interlocal agreement that included voting structures, pricing structures, demand shares and member agreements. Under this agreement, the board of directors for Cascade would be comprised of one elected representative from each member agency. All voting would be by a dual majority vote, meaning both a simple majority of members and a majority of weighted vote, proportional to water demand. All members would pay the same rates and had the option of turning control or ownership of their independent supply over to Cascade. In short, members would have the power.

With the interlocal agreement, proposed structure and government nonprofit status, Cascade was ready to move forward. Skyway and Bellevue, the first Cascade members, were soon joined by Seattle purveyors—Kirkland, Redmond, Tukwila, Mercer Island and Duvall, and Bryn Mawr/Skyway Water and Sewer District, Olympic View Water and Sewer District, and Woodinville Water District. Non-Seattle purveyors who joined included Issaquah, Covington Water District and the Sammamish Plateau Water and Sewer District.

As all the participants knew, part of the agreement included a stipulation that Cascade secure purveyors representing at least 75 percent of the volume of water members used to join Cascade—and relinquish individual Seattle contracts—by Nov. 15, 1999 to secure the contract offered by Seattle. By mid-1999, some agencies already had their governing bodies approve this agreement. Unfortunately, some felt it was in their best interests to continue purchasing water directly from Seattle and did not approve the agreement. That feeling was in part because there were areas of contention between the cities and the water districts, and in part because some were unsure what role of Bellevue, the largest member by far, would have in Cascade.

NEW LEADERS

Gwenn Maxfield, former chair of IWG, was hired as Cascade's interim General Manager and charged with taking the first steps for the fledgling agency. Those initial steps included hiring a full-time general manager, with other staff to be added for engineering, financial and administrative functions. The board directed Maxfield to launch a local search for the general manager, but a suitable candidate was not found, so Maxfield initiated a national search.

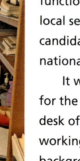

Cascade Director of Planning Michael Gagliardo

It was mid-spring of 1999 when the announcement for the Cascade general manager came across the desk of Michael Gagliardo, who at the time was working for the U.S. Conference of Mayors with a background in solid waste and water. After four years in Washington D.C., he was ready to try something different and this opportunity interested him. Following a phone interview with Maxfield, Gagliardo was brought out in May for interviews with Scott Thomasson of Redmond and Judy Nelson of Covington among others. After a series of interviews, meetings and a presentation at a reception, it was clear Cascade had found the right fit. Michael Gagliardo was hired to get Cascade organized and running.

As he understood the situation, the Interlocal Agreement had been approved, the Seattle contract had been approved and all member purveyors were in the process of and expected to ratify and adopt the agreements by the November deadline. But that wasn't actually the case.

In June, prior to his official August start date, Gagliardo returned to the Puget Sound area to attend a meeting to go over what he thought were details of his assignment. When he arrived for the meeting, there were five agencies represented only by their attorneys—no staff. These representatives of Shoreline and the Highline, Coal Creek, Soos Creek and Cedar River water districts had come to say their agencies were no longer participating with the creation of Cascade and left.

"It was clear to me that there was a very big divide between the cities and the districts," Gagliardo shared. "Sammamish Plateau Water and Sewer District and Covington Water District were in moratorium and needed water. The Tacoma Second Supply pipeline was still uncertain. Northshore and Woodinville Water Districts were hoping to get water from a deal with Everett and Weyerhaeuser. Gwenn was trying to hold them all together."

Gagliardo had moved his family to Mercer Island by August. He hired Pam Higbee to run the office, and the two of them were the entire Cascade staff for several years. From an office in the Bellfield Office Park in Bellevue, he went right to work. One of the first things he did was make the rounds to all the utilities that had opted out, meeting with each purveyor who was not a member at that time. When he asked them to sign the Interlocal Agreement and the Seattle contract, it became very apparent that he was trying to sell something that not everyone wanted. It seemed no district trusted Bellevue, which at the time was in the middle of that city's assumption of a portion of the Coal Creek Water District. Additionally, a provision in the formation requiring 75 percent of water volume meant if membership was not reached, and agreements with the Tacoma Second Supply Project were not yet finalized, currently committed members could withdraw from Cascade. The group had met in good faith together for three years and although it was well into the home stretch, things were beginning to fall apart.

While it was disappointing for many that the region lost an opportunity to have a regional water system, and hostilities continued over this "defection" for years, Cascade continued to move forward.

FACING THE CHALLENGE

The tight coalition—the "family"—was fracturing. By the Nov. 15, 1999 deadline only 51 percent of Seattle purveyors (Bellevue, Redmond, Kirkland, Mercer Island, Tukwila, Duvall and the Woodinville, Olympic View and Skyway/Bryn Mawr water districts) had signed. In addition, non-Seattle purveyors Issaquah, Covington Water and Sammamish Plateau Water and Sewer Districts had joined. It turned out that many districts decided to go with the devil they knew, Seattle, as opposed to the devil they didn't—Bellevue and Cascade. By not meeting 75 percent of suppliers' collective volume of water used meant the Seattle agreements wouldn't be offered and the water contract was off the table.

After the efforts fell apart, Seattle pursued separate negotiations with the water districts and with the cities. Ron Speers of Soos Creek Water and Sewer, one of the leaders who chose to remain with Seattle, said, "I know we were all in this together and we all wanted more clout. But after the first deal fell through, we wanted to remove the landlord-tenant relationship. Seattle offered those of us who stayed the opportunity to become part of what eventually was an operating board. I was its first chair. For us it was the better deal."

While it was disappointing for many that the region lost an opportunity to have a regional water system, and hostilities continued over this "defection" for years, Cascade continued to move forward.

On Nov. 16, 1999, one day after the offer expired, Cascade received a letter from Seattle Mayor Paul Schell stating that since Cascade had failed to reach the 75 percent threshold, Seattle was rejecting Cascade as the organization to meet future needs outside Seattle and was beginning a new governance process. Meanwhile in a memo, Lloyd Warren, Bellevue Utilities Manager, told the Bellevue City Council that, "it was expected that Cascade would approach Seattle to renegotiate the draft contract with modifications necessary to meet the changed interests of Cascade and Seattle."

This, in essence, brought discussions and decisions back to where they were at the beginning of the process in 1985. Most Cascade members interpreted Schell's letter as a reversal in policy from allowing suburban jurisdictions control of their own destiny to one which put Seattle back in charge of regional water supply decisions. It created a different relationship for Seattle and Cascade.

Cascade Board Members Jon Ault, Skyway, Lloyd Warren, Sammamish Plateau and Mary Alyce Burleigh, Kirkland

Prior to this point it was expected that Cascade would be the water supply agency that would be planning for the future of the region. Seattle would rest on its previous investments and take back supply from the new entity as it grew, making it a minor player in determining the future of supply. That had all changed with the failure of the 75% initiative. Now Seattle wasn't precluded from "competing" with Cascade to sell water to non-Cascade purveyors. And, Cascade did not control all of the supply in the region that Seattle didn't use for itself.

Cascade Chair Chuck Mosher, Bellevue Mayor, responded to Schell in a letter expressing deep concern with Seattle's direction and indicated that Cascade was formed and prepared to move ahead in the role of regional water supplier. The Cascade board met on Nov. 23, 1999 and expressed solidarity on approaching Seattle to continue the process and in any event collectively represent the interests of its members. A meeting was set for Mosher and Mayor Shell to begin that process.

Before the board were the following possible scenarios:
- Cascade will not enter into governance discussions as envisioned by Seattle, but would collectively negotiate directly with Seattle if such a process could be accomplished in a short time frame;
- If Cascade is unsuccessful in negotiations with Seattle, there is a

possibility that members who have historically used Seattle supply would legally pursue rights to access that supply in the future;
- Examine other supply options existing in the region including the Tacoma Second Supply, water rights that are being converted from industrial use in the Everett area, and reclaimed water which may be available from King County; and/or
- Develop a water supply strategy to address "water for people and water for fish."

NEW NEGOTIATIONS

Working with the Cascade board, Gagliardo was struggling to keep Cascade moving forward on two major fronts—water supply and public perception. Both were challenging for a staff of just one. The initial strategy was two-fold—to obtain a long term contract with Seattle for a fixed block of water from Seattle's current supplies, and to acquire access to new supplies to meet future needs of Cascade members. In 2000, Cascade began negotiating with Seattle on a declining block agreement for water supply. The challenge was that Seattle was going to decide what Cascade needed. There was no discussion regarding the amount of water and it included little room for growth.

"We knew it wasn't enough, especially since the Sammamish Plateau and Issaquah, our members, had not been part of the Seattle system so were not part of the amount Seattle would allow for Cascade," Gagliardo recalled, adding that, "Seattle kept the Eastside hostage for water." So Cascade turned to the south.

Tacoma's Second Supply Project was created for Covington, Tacoma, Lakehaven and others. Even though the Seattle City Council approved the agreement with Tacoma, Seattle's Diana Gale hadn't signed it. She wanted changes in the contract and said Tacoma could not move water through Seattle's system as it did not meet Seattle water quality standards—even though it met federal drinking water standards. Tacoma partners gave Seattle a date by which to sign. When they did not, Cascade hoped to get Seattle's capacity rights, but Tacoma took two-thirds of

> Working with the Cascade board, Gagliardo was struggling to keep Cascade moving forward on two major fronts—water supply and public perception. Both were challenging for a staff of just one.

Seattle's one-third and Covington, Lakehaven and others took the remainder.

That meant Gagliardo still had to find Cascade a new source. His efforts were supported by knowledgeable member staff, like Lloyd Warren of Bellevue, Sheldon Lynne of Issaquah, Scott Thomasson of Redmond and Erin Leonhart of Kirkland. Initial board members involved in Cascade's goals included: Bellevue's Chuck Mosher, as chair, Alan Merkle, Mercer Island; Alan Blanchard, Bryn Mawr/Lakeridge/Skyway; Steve Mullett and Jim Haggerton, Tukwila; Sants Contreras, Kirkland; Maureen Jewitt, Woodinville Water District; Thomas De Laat, Covington; Mark Cole, Duval; Patricia Meeker, Olympic View Water and Sewer; Rosemary Ives and Sharon Dorning, Redmond; and Steve Stevlingston, Sammamish Plateau Water and Sewer District.

And, while Seattle would sell Cascade water in a declining 30-year block, it was likely only enough to meet demand through 2010. Gagliardo hoped to establish a deal with Tacoma for the water, pipeline and transmission facilities needed for Issaquah and Sammamish. But, again, that was only good through about 2020. As water supplies usually take about 20 years to bring on line, the window was small for Cascade to secure its own long-term water source.

A key would be to determine how much water Cascade members really needed, so a demand forecast was undertaken. Each member submitted the amount of water it projected would be needed to meet its future demand, creating a plan for growth unlike the amount Seattle had calculated. Cascade added all the numbers together, but without adjusting for changes in the demand that began in 1992, after the region's drought. The numbers in Cascade's initial demand forecast were very high. At the same time, the methodology established in Cascade's Interlocal Agreements was beginning to generate Regional Capital

> "Water purveyors were worried growth in the region would outstrip supply."

Facilities Charges (RCFC) which provided income for the agency.

With the demand forecast numbers in hand, it was clear that two of Cascade members, Issaquah and the Sammamish Plateau, would need additional water for projected growth beyond what their groundwater could provide. As luck would have it, area developer Port Blakely was going to build The Highlands in Issaquah with a 24 inch transmission pipe to serve that area. Port Blakely reserved half of the capacity for the eventual Highlands and Talus developments, and transferred ownership of the pipeline to Issaquah. Some of the pipeline capacity was purchased by Cascade for water supply needs for the Sammamish Plateau and for Seattle/Bellevue water via the reservoir at Eastgate Park through Issaquah to the Plateau.

AND MORE PLAYERS GET INVOLVED

Meanwhile, King County was undertaking a planning process to ensure adequate water for the region's salmon recovery efforts under the Endangered Species Act that also met the requirements of the state's Growth Management Act. King County Executive Ron Sims convened a group to discuss and collaborate current and future regional water supply plans.

He acknowledged that with cities, districts and Seattle in the midst of heated negotiations, many perceived this as a power grab by King County, but "it wasn't," Sims recalled. "There were those water providers that wanted to build pipes and wanted them beyond the urban growth line. We were not going to move that line, so the table was set. Water purveyors were worried growth in the region would outstrip supply. Their concern was that the next generation would end up paying for this. If we had to invoke our authority to deal with water supply issues, we would have."

Seattle objected to Sims' planning, which fanned the fires. The Seattle

Times deemed the struggle "water wars." The Seattle Post Intelligencer, in its Feb. 11, 2000 editorial cartoon, depicted Sims and Schell in a "duel" over regional water. "The region's hostilities were with Seattle, not the county. They needed water but I kept asking 'at what price?'" Sims said. "It wasn't a power grab, it was a call for rational well thought out planning."

Also around this time, to resolve how water supply was planned for as a region, the three major water suppliers—Seattle, Tacoma and Everett—formed the Central Puget Sound Water Supply Forum to do regional water planning, and began the critical process of creating the first regional water supply outlook, which was published in 2001.

Cartoon originally published in the *Seattle Post Intelligencer* Feb. 11, 2000. © David Horsey/seattlepi.com

THE BEST LAID PLANS

Across the board, emotions ran high. In an effort to bring everyone together to focus on Cascade's future, Michael Gagliardo called an annual meeting for February 2000. He felt that since King County and Seattle were both talking about water supply—and since Cascade was a new regional water supplier—they should all join in a regional discussion. So, who better to address the issues, he thought, than regional leaders King County Executive Ron Sims and Seattle Mayor Paul Schell? New to the area, Gagliardo was not aware of the friction that existed between the two entities and indeed the two leaders on many fronts, including "water wars." So, while both leaders attended the meeting, spoke and were cordial, it was clear they did not see eye to eye on water, but they both believed in the future of water planning.

A second annual meeting was equally unique. Cascade had been working with noted water attorney Jim Waldo, Governor Gary Locke's regional water advisor. Waldo secured the Governor as a speaker at Cascade's Feb. 28, 2001 annual meeting, scheduled for the Space Needle at the Seattle Center. However, about two hours before the event was to take place, the region was hit with a major earthquake, and the governor was unable to attend. Waldo stepped in to talk about the future of water, something Cascade, despite natural and political issues, still needed more than a year after its initial agreement failed… with the clock still ticking.

4.
DIVING FOR WATER

The goals of Cascade Water Alliance were to secure a long-term water supply and be an equal player among the Central Puget Sound region's water entities. The two goals went hand in hand, but to get there Cascade faced some major decisions along the way.

Cascade signed an initial "block" contract with Seattle as the major components of its water system. It would go into effect in January 2004. The Seattle block contract provided 30.3 million gallons per day through 2024.

Still, supply for additional future demands particularly of non-Seattle system purveyor members like Covington, Issaquah and the Sammamish Plateau were undetermined. Covington would receive additional supply by assuming a portion of the Seattle share of the Tacoma Second Supply Project in addition to that which it already owned. The Plateau, which was under a building moratorium, was expecting substantial new development in the future. It was projected that the purchase of water from the Tacoma Second Supply Project partners would provide for increased demand in the Plateau, as well as Issaquah and other Seattle system purveyor members. The Tacoma contract portion of Cascade's 2004 Transmission and Supply Plan afforded four million gallons per day of permanent water and six million gallons a day of temporary water.

However, since some of the Tacoma supply was not permanent, Cascade still needed to find a long-term water source. Further, Cascade needed to find a way to get the Tacoma water to the Eastside. A pipeline was envisioned at a capital cost of $67-$70 million. Cascade could also acquire the Bellevue-Issaquah Pipeline (BIP) under construction that would initially transport Seattle water.

In the late 1990s, the ongoing issues over water supply continued. Further impacting negotiations and discussions was Cascade's depleting membership. Mercer Island withdrew, as it was no longer growing and the city determined the existing contract with Seattle was adequate for that city. Woodinville, working to obtain water from the Weyerhaeuser water right, also left. And, the City of Duvall, citing lack of financial resource, also pulled out of Cascade. That meant that just eight members remained, but those members' need for water was still critical. One option was emerging at exactly the right time.

The powerhouse

THE LAKE TAPPS OPTION EMERGES

The history of Lake Tapps started in the early 1900s with one of the region's first hydro-electric operations. Puget Sound Energy's (PSE) White River Project in east Pierce County, a dynamic 12-mile system of flumes, diversions, pipes and valves to flood four small lakes into one reservoir. It was called Lake Tapps—as some old-timers claim—for the Tacoma and Puget Power System (TAPPS). The reservoir was 4.5 square miles of surface area and more than 45 miles of complex shoreline, with many inlets, peninsulas and islands, held in place by a series of 15 dikes.

Today's Puget Sound Energy (PSE) then known as Puget Sound Power and Light, sold the land around the reservoir in 1954 to the Lake Tapps

Right: The powerhouse, its construction and the turbines inside

Below: Lake Tapps Development Company brochure

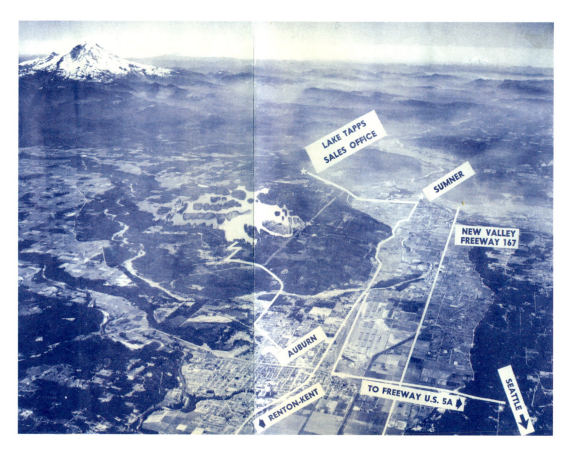

Development Corporation. Deeds came with the stipulation that the project may "draw the reservoir down to any level and use the waters thereof for the operations of the White River generating plant and to abandon said storage reservoir at any time, all without the liability for the damage suffered by the Grantee or anyone claiming through or under the Grantee." The area around the reservoir was developed and homes were built and sold.

PSE was then producing 55 megawatts of power, and the lake was often lowered to perform maintenance, inspect dikes and provide water

Drawn down for improvements in 2015

> "People asked if we were just going to walk away and leave. Of course, this could not nor would not be done, but residents were terribly concerned about the future of their lake."

for power. In 1962, PSE was ordered by the Federal Energy Regulatory Commission (FERC) to license the White River Project. FERC had required some PSE projects be licensed, others not. Ed Shield, then Puget's Director of Power Generation Group at White River, said the Supreme Court agreed that the White River did not need to be licensed since commerce was not conducted on the river. But in the 1980s, FERC again ordered PSE to license the Lake Tapps operations.

What followed was decades of appeals, filings and waiting. By 1992, FERC was requesting still more information about this project, and PSE requested permission to build fish screens ahead of license issuance. The fish screens were constructed in the White River flow line.

In 1997, the Muckleshoot Indian Tribe, the Puyallup Tribe of Indians and others appealed the FERC license. The next year, PSE, the US Fish and Wildlife Service, the National Marine Fisheries Service, the Washington State Department of Ecology and the Washington Department of Fish and Wildlife filed requests for rehearing on the licensing conditions.

PSE mitigation requirements for the license would cost as much as $6.6 million—more annually than the revenue generated by the project. Then, to make issues even more complicated, in March of 1998, the Puget Sound Chinook Salmon was proposed for listing as an Endangered Species by the National Marine Fisheries Service. This fish was prevalent in the White River.

White River Project Superintendent Gene Galloway, who like his father worked at PSE his entire career, knew every aspect of the system. He, along with several others, realized federal requirements could mean the end of the project. Ed Shield agreed, knowing PSE simply could not make an economic go of the White River project if it accepted the license. Shield and others began the process of decommissioning the project. "People asked if we were just going to walk away and leave," Shield recalls. "Of course, this could not nor would not be done, but [Lake Tapps] residents were terribly concerned about the future of their lake." Without ongoing operations, Lake Tapps could return to a mudflat.

Gary Nomensen of PSE briefed Pierce County's Councilmember Jan Shabo and then Executive Doug Southerland that it didn't pencil out for PSE to go ahead with the FERC project. PSE did, however, want to work with Pierce County to help determine the future of the lake.

RESIDENTS STEP UP

State Senator Pam Roach

One of those Lake Tapps residents happened to be Shawn Bunney, counsel to the Pierce County Council, who advised on water related issues. Bunney was working on the Tri-County Endangered Species Act response and was well versed in water issues when he became aware of the situation. In early February 1999, State Senator Pam Roach read about the issue in a Valley Daily News newspaper article, and Lake Tapps resident Kirk Shuler said he heard a news helicopter flying overhead one day and later that night saw the story on television. Others began to get wind of the news as well that PSE was shutting down operations.

Roach, a dedicated, feisty, action-oriented legislator from Auburn knew action was needed. She was but one legislator, and couldn't do it all by herself. Her approach was to go to the people, let them know what was going on and get them involved. "You win by fighting back," she said. Roach, who had a history of making things happen, had already had fought an environmental effort to stop sewage sludge (biosolids) from being sprayed as fertilizer in the area. Years before, she had stopped the siting of a county incinerator that was proposed adjacent to the elementary school her son Dan (currently Pierce County Council Chair) attended.

> Knowing that community involvement was once again critical, Roach sent out bright orange postcards for a public meeting to be held on Thursday evening Feb. 25, 1999 at the Emerald Hills Elementary School in Bonney Lake. The call to action was "Let's Save Lake Tapps!"

Knowing that community involvement was once again critical, Roach sent out bright orange postcards for a public meeting to be held on Thursday evening Feb. 25, 1999 at the Emerald Hills Elementary School in Bonney Lake. The call to action was "Let's Save Lake Tapps!"

The orange post card was a rallying cry that did the trick. More than 700 residents attended the meeting —so many that the fire marshal had to turn people away. Everyone had a lot at stake—their homes, their lives, their property values—and, for some that meant their retirement or financial security.

She recalls the emotion and the action-oriented sentiment of the meeting. "It was a game changer," she says of the meeting. "If we didn't do anything, who knows where we'd be today? As it was, after the meeting, I said 'We need leaders and if you are interested, follow me to the library.' And they did." Kirk Shuler was one of those who came. He helped find leaders among the many who came forward to volunteer, to write letters and be ground support.

Residents today acknowledge that the effort to save Lake Tapps would not have had the impact and the impetus it had without Pam Roach. "She got the whole thing started with a very emotional pitch and got volunteers enlisted that night. She pushed us hard. She was working for us. She was instrumental in saving our lake," recalls resident Ken Castile.

Following the initial organizational meeting, two groups emerged with the same goal of saving the lake but taking different directions. One was Friends of Lake Tapps, headed by Kirk Shuler and Don Fisher, who advocated for bringing in legal counsel to advise residents of their rights under environmental regulations. The other was the Save Lake Tapps Coalition which was led by Dennis Brown who wanted to review other options.

> "Everyone wanted solutions for different things and different reasons," Hilyer explained. "But they all came together for a common purpose…to save the lake."

Pierce County Council member Jan Shabo committed to starting a task force in 1999. She brought in Rhonda Hilyer, the skilled facilitator who seven years earlier had guided the beginnings of Cascade, to help the community move forward.

Hilyer said there were 38 different interests represented at the table, including homeowners, PSE, elected officials, the US Army Corps of Engineers, cities, Pierce County, realtors, business representatives, schools, fire districts, recreational users and the Puyallup Watershed Council.

"Everyone wanted solutions for different things and different reasons," Hilyer explained. "But they all came together for a common purpose…to save the lake." The group called itself the Lake Tapps Task Force (LTTF) and embraced a bipartisan leadership throughout the process, ultimately finding some tremendous leaders with unique strengths.

The angst began to disappear once the task force forged a bond. "Failure is Not an Option" became the group's mantra. Various committees reviewed dozens of options, their feasibility and their cost. Others developed modeling to determine how the lake levels functioned. And, everyone knew that whatever solution was arrived at also had to fulfill Endangered Species Act (ESA) and federal regulations.

More than 34 initial proposals were put forward regarding potential future uses for Lake Tapps. The LTTF agreed to consider 13 of the most viable options. Across the board, the top priorities that emerged were using the lake as a municipal drinking water source and making sure the reservoir would be maintained consistently.

Lake Tapps Task Force mantra

FAILURE: Never an Option.

Pierce County Executive John Ladenburg and the Lake Tapps Task Force

CASCADE GETS DOWN TO BUSINESS

Meanwhile, in Bellevue, Cascade Water Alliance had yet to meet its goal of providing a long-term water supply commitment to members after Seattle's supply began to decline in 2024. Knowing it needed all of those remaining two decades to permit and construct any water supply project, it was critical to get a viable option.

Water supply was also a topic Bob King, an engineer with HDR Inc., was working on as a consultant for Puget Sound Energy in 1999-2000. He was developing an initial water supply concept for Lake Tapps in Pierce County. King knew that PSE was in the licensing process of the FERC, and was aware FERC requirements were making the energy project impractical. PSE had already approached Seattle and Tacoma to see if they had any interest in water supply and even purchasing the project for water. They had both turned down acquisition of Lake Tapps as unfeasible. Near the end of 1998 and early 1999, King knew Cascade Water Alliance was looking for water and he wondered if it might be a great fit for the two utilities.

Chuck Mosher of Bellevue said Cascade's plan for acquiring Lake Tapps was a saving grace. It meant Cascade would have water. But equally important was the fact that having Lake Tapps would give Cascade political leverage.

PSE inquired whether Cascade might be interested in the development of a water supply component on the Lake Tapps hydropower facility. The Cascade board expressed interest in the water supply portion of the project for which PSE would seek a water right, and began to pursue an agreement with PSE, deeming it "critical to the future of Cascade." This was a big step in reaching its goal, but was also the first significant financial commitment Cascade would be considering since its formation.

With this potential water source on the table, Cascade Water Alliance representatives started to come to the LTTF meetings. Residents didn't know Cascade and the community started to get nervous. Lake Tapps resident Leon Stucki recalls, "We were between a rock and a hard place. They wanted water. Here it was. But we didn't know them and we didn't trust them or Bellevue."

Cities surrounding Lake Tapps were also concerned. City leaders of Auburn, Bonney Lake, Buckley and Sumner feared that "their water" would be taken elsewhere and that their citizens might not have sufficient water for the future. Bonney Lake had already looked at the feasibility of purchasing the lake and it simply did not make fiscal sense. Additionally, Auburn had groundwater supply, hydraulically connected to the White River. The city had already conducted extensive studies to determine future impacts and explore the feasibility of being a regional water provider.

PSE decided that it should apply for a municipal water right for Lake Tapps. It would continue to operate the system for power, and could provide Cascade water before it reached the power generating turbines. PSE sought water rights to divert water from the White River, store it in Lake Tapps and pump it for municipal water use. Filing the three water

White River

rights permit applications gave PSE seniority over anyone else, effectively making sure no one else could file. Ed Shield, the Director of Power Generation Group at White River, said PSE applied for the potable water right even though it did not want to be in the water supply business, but it knew Cascade did.

Chuck Mosher of Bellevue said Cascade's plan for acquiring Lake Tapps was a saving grace. It meant Cascade would have water. But equally important was the fact that having Lake Tapps would give Cascade political leverage. Cascade would be at the table with the other major water providers in the region making decisions regarding regional water policy now and in the future. Their two-fold goal would be realized.

APPEALS AND DEALS

The first water right was issued to PSE in 2003, and was immediately appealed by the Tribes, who were worried about low instream flows and the impact on salmon, and by Auburn, concerned that the city's groundwater could be affected. By 2003, FERC's draft license conditions were considered so onerous that PSE rejected any license and stopped generating hydroelectric power in 2004.

PSE rejected the FERC license in late 2003 and the Pollution Control Hearing Board remanded the water rights back to the Department of Ecology for reconsideration. The "baseline" for granting the water rights was with hydro and with no FERC license. With no hydro, this baseline for a decision was no longer valid.

In order to keep things moving, Cascade and PSE came back to the table and worked together to begin the process of transferring the White River project to Cascade. The bulk of the negotiating for Cascade was conducted by Gagliardo and Cascade's general counsel Mike Ruark. Cascade board member Grant Degginger of Bellevue, himself an attorney, brought in Joel Gordon, an attorney with Buck & Gordon, to work on the real estate portions of the sale of Lake Tapps from PSE to Cascade.

Cascade developed a term sheet with PSE, then set out to complete the real estate deal. According to Gordon, there was a tremendous number of moving parts with layer after layer of complications. But Cascade eventually finalized the term sheet, which was challenging considering everything PSE had done on the project over the last 100 years.

LTTF brochure about saving Lake Tapps

One key issue was the need for potential environmental cleanup of the site. While PSE didn't want to give Cascade a blank check, the two parties came to a workable agreement that if Cascade found any contamination or other problems, PSE would work to get it resolved. PSE was responsible for any known releases. PSE also retained ownership of certain areas of known contamination, and granted Cascade necessary easements.

While things were looking good for Cascade, the State Department of Ecology had still not granted the needed water right. The White River basin is considered a "closed" basin, meaning no additional water can be taken from it or water rights issued for that water unless there is overriding consideration

> "...With Lake Tapps we evened the playing field and had leverage. Cascade may never need to build out or use water from Lake Tapps, but it's there if the region ever needs it. As result, Lake Tapps turned the table in the region's water supply discussions."

of public interest (OCPI). It was the possibility of an OCPI that was the basis of Cascade preparing and Ecology evaluating water rights for use of Lake Tapps. And, Cascade wanted to have the real estate transaction completed to coincide with the issuance of the water right. It also wanted to have agreements in place with the Puyallup Tribe of Indians, the Muckleshoot Indian Tribe, the homeowners and the cities. Without agreements and an eventual water right, Cascade would end up with a lake it couldn't use.

After extensive negotiations, Cascade completed the purchase and bought the White River-Lake Tapps project in December 2009. The purchase price of $30 million was down from the term sheet amount of $37 million prior to the final deal. Cascade hired legal, environmental and engineering firms to perform due diligence, going through 100 years of documents to assess obligations. When Cascade bought the White River-Lake Tapps project, it purchased a project subject to all agreements that had been put in place over 100 years. This included property rights, drainage, road easements and other agreements.

"It was the most amazing transaction I have ever worked on in terms of the complexities and the number of issues," said Gordon. "There were 130 pieces of property, seven miles of canals, a lake, a power plant and dikes. We almost got derailed over the dikes and what the Washington State Dam Safety Office would require.

"Cascade had its water source. This would totally change negotiation dynamics with Seattle and Tacoma," Gordon noted. "We would have an alternate source of water. If Seattle and Tacoma didn't sell water to Cascade a large share of their supply would sit unsold. Previously, they had had us boxed into a corner on a very uneven playing field. With Lake Tapps we evened the playing field and had leverage. Cascade may

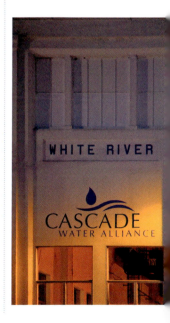

Cascade completed the purchase of the White River Lake Tapps project in 2009

never need to build out or use water from Lake Tapps, but it's there if the region ever needs it. As result, Lake Tapps turned the table in the region's water supply discussions."

Cascade now owned the entire White River Project. Water came into Lake Tapps in two places. A diversion structure on the White River near the Buckley routes water into a flowline which empties into the east side of the lake. On the west side of the reservoir, water had originally been routed to the Dieringer Powerhouse to generate hydroelectricity, after which the water was returned to the White River about 20 miles downstream from the diversion dam. Although today there is no power generation, the water continues to be diverted and returned to the river through the former hydropower infrastructure. The level of the reservoir can be lowered in the fall and winter for maintenance and repairs, and aquatic plant management. Additionally, since 1948 the US Army Corps of Engineers has owned and operated a fish trap at the diversion structure on the White River, which catches salmon migrating upstream. The fish are driven by truck and released upriver of Mud Mountain Dam which blocks salmon migration. This technique is called a "trap and haul system." But all of that water flow and fish traps aside, for Cascade, Lake Tapps' eventual use was to be a municipal water supply that would meet the growing demands of its members.

FORECASTING THE FUTURE

Predicting demand is not easy. Cascade's 2004 projections were based on what the individual Cascade members thought they might eventually need. According to engineer Bob King everyone in the region thought demand would continue to escalate as growth continued and that a

Enjoying Lake Tapps (photo on right by Janice Thomas)

significant amount of water would be needed. Population and the economy were booming and demand would increase, conventional wisdom held.

Chuck Clarke, then head of Seattle Public Utilities, had negotiated the deal with Cascade for its first block contract. He also thought Cascade's demand projections weren't accurate when Seattle couldn't validate them under its forecast models. "We questioned their numbers and thought their projections just weren't justified. I spoke with Bellevue leaders about the numbers and offered to cut a deal and keep them part of the Seattle system but I was told no—twice," Clarke recalled.

But, when King and others added up all the members' individual demands, the numbers didn't match up to what was really being used. Cascade's projections were based on regional growth and high per capita water use. Altogether, Cascade's contracts with Seattle and Tacoma provided a minimum of 34.3 million gallons per day (mgd) and a temporary maximum of 40.3 mgd. Ed Cebron, of Financial Consulting Solutions Group (FCSG) said the numbers Cascade had received from its members weren't realistic and hadn't been reconciled to actual demands. With so much water at stake, Cascade was charged with adjusting its projected demands to line up with what members were actually using.

As it turns out, history would show all water utilities were over forecasting demands by varying degrees by the mid-2010s and that demand had been dropping for some time.

Cascade CEO
Chuck Clarke

CREATING A ROUTE

After completing the 2004 Transmission and Supply Plan, which used the initial demand forecasting, Cascade began the process of designing a route to bring the Lake Tapps water to its members by 2024. This plan called for building a pipeline from Tacoma's second supply pipeline through Covington to Lake Youngs in Pierce County though Seattle's pipe. Cascade asked Seattle if this would work. The answer was that all water must meet Seattle's quality standards, which would require the Lake Tapps water receive some sort of treatment. Cascade then asked

Seattle if it could use Tacoma water and wheel it within the Seattle system. Again, the answer was no because of Seattle's water standards.

With water quality issues stymieing the effort to use Seattle systems, Cascade looked for different options. The next idea was to bring Tacoma water to the Issaquah Highlands and Talus, by constructing a pipeline under SR 900. Cascade would use the Seattle block allotment for its other members.

Cascade got to work with the full and active support of the Cascade board. Gagliardo hired Dennis Fields as a project engineer and Mike Brent to develop and implement conservation programs. The draft plan was to build a central line from Tacoma's Second Supply pipeline to Lake Youngs; a northern line from Lake Youngs to Issaquah; and a southern line from Lake Tapps to the second supply line. Routes were in design and Cascade acquired real estate to put a pipeline in SR 900 while the State Department of Transportation was doing work there. Their plan was coming together, but it was extensive and expensive.

Others in the region continued to question their demand numbers and need for such a venture. Plus, Cascade did not yet have a water right for municipal water right for Lake Tapps. What it did have were hostile neighbors on all sides, the Tribes, homeowners and four communities. The goal was in sight, but it seemed the battle continued for Cascade.

Opposite: Lake Tapps (photo by Janice Thomas)

Below: Cascade Water Resource Manager Mike Brent

5.
CASCADE'S TODDLER YEARS

While the effort may have started nearly two decades before, recent progress for Cascade was at seemingly breakneck speed. In fact, so much had happened so fast that Cascade board members decided to slow down, take a step back and evaluate next steps...

First, Cascade had acquired water from Seattle and Tacoma for the immediate future. Second, Cascade was buying a reservoir with water supply for the long term. And third, it was on its way to figuring out how to get that water to members and their residents with a pipeline transmission. Cascade and its members were realizing the dream of determining their own destiny with a voice and a vote. But, as any fledgling agency, it was a little wobbly on its new 'toddler' legs.

Cascade Board Chair Grant Degginger, Mayor of Bellevue, and John Marchione, Mayor of Redmond, conferred with long time project champion and now board member Lloyd Warren. Warren had retired from Bellevue and was a commissioner representing the Sammamish Plateau Water and Sewer District on the board. Degginger, Marchione and Warren asked themselves some serious questions. Was the organization ready to move forward? Was it staffed appropriately? How should it grow to maximize its efforts? Was it the most efficient government operation it could be? Was it ready to tackle next steps?

To this point, the individuals working on this project had been primarily lawyers and engineers. Much had been done internally and with the member staff. A major pipeline had been drawn and proposed, and the needed real estate had been purchased. Degginger knew it was time to turn to the community and engage them in what was to come

next. He and Marchione knew that there was value in having the public understand the need for a pipeline, especially during a public process to obtain environmental impact statements and franchises. Public outreach was critical, but how to get it? In 2005, they turned to local community relations duo Betty Spieth and Sarah Langton to work with Cascade's newly created Public Affairs Committee and direct that outreach effort. Degginger, as chair, asked Marchione to head up this group. Its charter was to begin Cascade's critical work of identifying and reaching out to key community stakeholders to increase awareness and understanding of Cascade, connect in the community and build vital relationships with those who might be deciding Cascade's fate.

Cascade Board Members Grant Degginger, John Marchione and Lloyd Warren

"We put a stakeholder outreach process together," said Langton. "We went out to groups and asked who knew what Cascade was. No one raised a hand. There was a lot of work to do."

Langton and Spieth also staffed the Public Affairs Committee for Marchione. In early 2006, Langton and Spieth recommended board members from Cascade speak to the relatively new Leadership Eastside program, a group aimed at grooming the Eastside's future leaders.

"For the first time, Cascade leaders articulated their vision for the future," said Speith. Board members Mary Alyce Burleigh of Kirkland, Lloyd Warren, Joe Folkner of Issaquah and Degginger presented a case for Cascade that was so articulate and moving that Speith called it one of the most inspirational she'd experienced in all her public policy work. In sharing their dream and goal for deciding the region's own destiny and ensuring water for the area's future, Speith said "They captured the essence of Cascade [for] each future leader in that room."

Cascade Board Member Mary Alyce Burleigh

Using that momentum, the Public Affairs Committee wanted to develop a comprehensive outreach plan that would help pave the way to public knowledge and acceptance of its plans. Cascade wasn't just an anonymous government agency anymore, it was creating a public persona.

REFOCUSING ON THE VISION

In the waning days of December 2006, on a proverbial dark and stormy night before Christmas Eve, Cascade board members met to do some "dining and dreaming." It was so important that they were all willing to come together during that busy time of the year to reimagine the future. Cascade members were concerned that, as it currently was staffed, Cascade might not yet be up to the task. There was agreement that the organization needed a reboot, to be refocused. The goal was to clarify and revitalize the vision for Cascade's future. Members created a wish list of headlines they'd like to see in the future.

The result? By all accounts, magic happened at that late December retreat. Together that evening, members charted a reenergized path toward realizing their vision and goal, which had never wavered—a voice and a vote in water and to be able to determine their own future. This helped the board solidify to work together for the region. Cascade

Agenda for Dinner and Dreaming

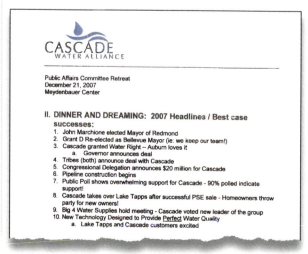

had an active board, ran a lean and efficient organization and made outstanding use of members' utility staffs. What became apparent to all was that additional and perhaps different sets of skills were needed to move the organization forward to complete the work ahead.

Degginger turned to a former Bellevue staff member he knew well and trusted for help. Ed Oberg had just retired from the City of Bellevue and was a master at organizational administration.

Oberg listened to Cascade's concerns and accepted the challenge of examining the needs of the growing Cascade organization. It was clear that a CEO was needed, and Oberg accepted that role until a permanent one could be found. He quickly brought in two key retired City of Bellevue employees, Paul Bader and Andi Dash, to get the house in administrative order. Michael Gagliardo became director of planning, making the most of his essential strengths. Oberg did a request for proposals for a strategic management consultant to take an objective look at the internal organization. Of the six respondents it received, Cascade chose Moss Adams to do an assessment. That assessment pointed to several areas that needed attention.

The first was that Cascade needed "infrastructure" to manage, among other things, the day to day administrative policies and procedures any organization must follow. Gagliardo had been running the organization virtually by himself and focusing on what he did best—planning for water supply. Both he and the board knew he couldn't do it all, certainly not anymore. Cascade needed strong professionals and needed them right away.

Towards that end, the board hired a Finance and Business Administrative Director—Scott Hardin, who then added Business Manager Chris Paulucci to the growing team. Hardin was an ideal fit for the organization and immediately began creating and implementing that needed infrastructure.

The second need was on the legal front, since long time general counsel Mike Ruark of Inslee Best was retiring. Cascade expanded Gordon' Derr's duties (now VanNess Feldman) to include serving as Cascade's general legal counsel, with T.C. Richmond as lead. It also continued its relationship with attorneys John Parness for construction, and Steve Winterbauer for employment issues.

SMOOTHING OUT THE BUMPS

Third, public perception issues continued to plague Cascade. Some water purveyors still said they didn't see the need for the entity. It was clear that Cascade faced more struggles with future plans to construct a pipeline and begin operations around Lake Tapps. Additional communications, community and government relations support were brought in to garner public support.

Then Oberg tackled operational issues. After talking to other water suppliers in the region, the message about demand remained consistent—water demand was down despite population growth. Those previous demand forecasts from 2004 were called into question when water experts told Oberg that Cascade's demand numbers were still not realistic and did not warrant all that was being planned. Part of the issue was that members themselves had originally stipulated the amount of water they'd need. With no restraints and no cost responsibilities, each had given a wild estimate and there had been no testing of their assumptions. Clearly now, the amount greatly exceeded need. But even then, HDR, FCSG and Gagliardo had tried to moderate the numbers in preparation of the 2004 Transmission and Supply Plan, unfortunately with little success. In what had been a good economy with lots of growth, the demand from the members had not been closely questioned. Now they were. About this time Dennis Fields left Cascade.

Another glitch became apparent when Oberg began exploring the Lake Tapps situation more thoroughly and determined it was doubtful the pipeline project could be done by the time the water from Seattle would run out. The project was now significantly more costly than envisioned an estimated $300 million. But, if water experts were right and demand was way down from Cascade projections, and if other water suppliers were experiencing reduced demand as well—these providers in the region had a lot of water and might want to sell it. The need for

Opposite:
Proposed pipeline from Lake Tapps to Cascade

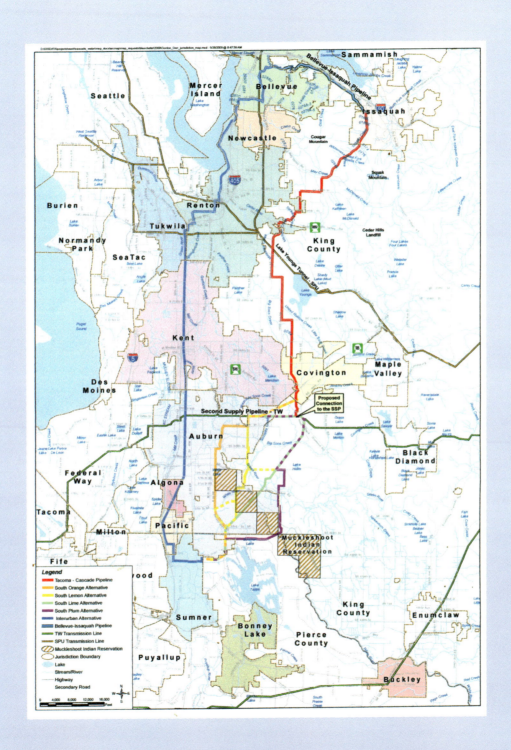

> "The world had changed since this plan had first been envisioned," Oberg reflected. It seemed Cascade needed to catch its breath before moving ahead with Lake Tapps.

building a pipeline from Lake Tapps might not be necessary as quickly as originally envisioned.

"Plus, I was worried about the political and community implications of building the pipeline, from neighborhoods to noise—and none of that outreach or permitting work had been done," said Oberg. "There was no franchise with King County, Renton or Covington and no permits had even been applied for. No political bases had been covered or any public outreach work done. No approvals, no groundwork laid, no champions but Cascade members. There wasn't anyone who had their finger on pulse of demand on a plan to meet that high demand. No one had asked the hard questions. And it was to be built in a year!

"The world had changed since this plan had first been envisioned," Oberg reflected. It seemed Cascade needed to catch its breath before moving ahead with Lake Tapps.

As a stop gap action, Oberg got the green light from the board to buy water on an interim basis from Seattle, which excess water to sell. Besides ensuring water supply, this outreach would also create an ally of Seattle when Cascade applied for its water right. Chuck Clarke, still head of Seattle Public Utilities, said Seattle would sell some of its surplus water

Cascade staff

Chuck Clarke at Barrier Structure on White River

to Cascade, giving it time to determine Plan B. Along with the security of water and the gift of time, this option was far less expensive than building a pipeline. With all those factors in mind, the Cascade pipeline project was put on hold.

BUILDING CREDIBILITY

Now Oberg could move on to the next task, the search for a permanent CEO for the Cascade board. Degginger and Marchione wanted SPU's director Chuck Clarke, who eventually agreed to come to Cascade in December 2008. Clarke had tremendous insight into what needed to be done, outstanding utility knowledge and the political sense of how to get things done. He was personable, knowledgeable and trustworthy in a utility ditch or in a boardroom. He wasn't a fan of bureaucracy—a perfect fit for Cascade. Chuck brought with him from Seattle Linda Moreno, who quickly became the hub around which Cascade functioned efficiently.

Most of the items of the board's 2006 "dining and dreaming" items could be checked off the list, recalled Oberg, wrapping up his work at Cascade. "When I left Cascade it was a better place. Fewer moving parts,

There was work to be done, trust to be established and bridges to be built, one stakeholder at a time.

more details nailed down. We reached out, communicated, coordinated and talked and got the right people in right jobs. But while Cascade had managed to deal with the potential pipeline and construction by closing it down [for now], we really needed to mend fences around the lake and quickly."

With the right people in place and the pipeline to bring Lake Tapps water to Cascade on hold, Cascade turned to establishing agreements with three critical stakeholders who could have major impacts on the project. Gagliardo, Degginger and Warren were already negotiating with the first stakeholders, the Muckleshoot Tribe of Indians and the Puyallup Indian Tribe, regarding instream flows on the White River for fish.

Next were the homeowners around Lake Tapps. Unfortunately, Gagliardo and the homeowners were at a standoff from previous dealings. Cascade assumed the PSE/Homeowner agreements with the purchase of Lake Tapps, but the homeowners didn't trust that assumption would actually happen. The crux of the issue was the priority of how the water would be allocated. Homeowners wanted recreational lake levels to take precedence over minimum instream flows and water supply.

Finally, the four cities around the lake—Auburn, Bonney Lake, Buckley and Sumner—were still angry with Cascade board members. The opposition that began with PSE's first water rights application in 2003 continued, and their distrust meant they would not work with Cascade and would oppose them at every turn.

Support or at least neutrality from the three critical stakeholders at Lake Tapps—the Tribes, the homeowners and the four cities—was essential as Cascade pursued its water right for municipal water use of this reservoir. There was work to be done, trust to be established and bridges to be built, one stakeholder at a time.

Opposite: Lake Tapps (photo by Sky-Pix)

6.
CASCADE'S NEW NEIGHBORS—
THE TRIBES

Cascade knew that any relationship with the Tribes began by understanding how the Tribes saw the value of the White River. For them it provided a major transportation corridor for the most important of all things—the fish.

The Puget Sound Chinook Salmon had been listed as Endangered Species in 1998, Bull Trout in 1999, and then Coho was named as a species of concern shortly after. Steelhead were listed in 2006. In order to support and protect these fish, the law stated existing fisheries must be maintained and enhanced. The US Army Corps of Engineers built a fish trap in the White River in the 1940s. Beginning as a temporary facility to secure and save fish, it had become permanent but was inadequate to do the job, and all parties knew it.

Cascade also knew that any step forward regarding Lake Tapps could impact the fish and must secure support from and approval of the Muckleshoot Indian Tribe and the Puyallup Tribe of Indians. Discussions had already begun with the Tribal representatives and Cascade's Michael Gagliardo, Board Chair Grant Degginger, Bellevue Mayor, attorney Mike Ruark and board member Lloyd Warren all at the table. The four year negotiations effort began in 2005 with the Puyallup Tribe. The Muckleshoot were brought into the discussions later. The conversations continued through 2008 and focused on the technical instream flow issues.

Opposite:
White River

Fish in the trap

Degginger said, "The Tribes were nervous and distrustful of Cascade buying the lake and the potential water right. They wanted to keep their fisheries' interest strong and restore habitat by keeping water in the river. They each had treaty rights. The municipal water right was a less intrusive use than power generation—the question was how do we manage their needs, our needs and recreational needs? How much could we give back to the instream flows?"

Historically, Puget Coast Power Company (which became the Puget Sound Power and Light Company and is now PSE), through an 1896 claim, had vesting rights from Pierce County and King County Superior Court, granting the power producer the right to divert up to 2,000 cubic feet per second (cfs) from the river to Lake Tapps, as long as a mandatory minimum flow of 30 cfs was left in the White River below the diversion structure. This essentially dewatered the 21 miles known as Reservation Reach, from the barrier dam to the tailrace. This had always been a sticking point with the Tribes who felt the amount of water left in the river was insufficient for fish.

In 1986, a settlement was made between PSE and the Muckleshoots, requiring PSE leave a minimum of 130 cfs in the river. PSE went on to build a hatchery and reimbursed the Muckleshoots for operating costs as well.

In the early 1990s, FERC began its process of issuing a license for PSE hydropower production. FERC recommendations for instream flows included adjustments as a result of the listing of the Chinook salmon as an Endangered Species, and became progressively higher over time. During this time, the National Oceanographic and Atmospheric Administration (NOAA) told the US Army Corps of Engineers (Corps) to establish flows in an interim operating agreement as the FERC proceeded. Those became the flows used until the settlement agreement was reached.

Saving fish at the fish trap

> "The overriding concern was that the Tribes wanted more water in the river," said Gagliardo. "But there were other issues as well—such as Tribal fishing rights and preserving the Tribes' culture with respect."

In 2000, PSE applied for a water right that was eventually issued in July 2003 by the State Department of Ecology (DOE.) However, it was promptly appealed by the Muckleshoot and Puyallup Tribes, Auburn, Puyallup, Buckley and others to the Pollution Control Hearings Board (PCHB). The appeal sat for some time. In 2004 PSE announced it would not accept the FERC license. This is when PSE stopped generating power at White River and gave the hatchery it built to Muckleshoot. With this change, the Pollutions Control Hearing Board remanded the pending 2003 water right back to the State Department of Ecology. It cited that the pending right was based on hydropower production and now that there wouldn't be any, the water right had to be redone.

In the years that ensued, and as Cascade got ready to purchase the system from PSE, Ecology requested new recommendations. Once Cascade decided to purchase the lake, about mid-2005, Tribal discussions immediately focused on flow regime—instream flows, ramping rates and maximum diversions. "The overriding concern was that the Tribes wanted more water in the river," said Gagliardo. "But there were other issues as well—such as Tribal fishing rights and preserving the Tribes' culture with respect."

Minimum flows were a critical issue and were set based roughly on 50 percent median historic flows, adjusted every two to four weeks to mimic natural hydrology, with a scientific basis. Generally, these were higher flows than set by the National Oceanographic and Atmospheric Administration (NOAA) except in August and September.

Ramping rates were also an important issue. "As you divert water into the lake it changes the amount in the river. As flows increase water tends to move out, into side channels. As it decreases, it flows back into the main channel," Gagliardo explained. "The problem comes in those

Swans on Lake Tapps (photo by Janice Thomas)

side areas that can be isolated when the water moves out of the side channels. Those areas are critical for habitat, spawning, eggs, juveniles, and must be protected so they do not dry out or dewater. Fish follow water so we can't increase or decrease too fast—or ramping up or down." Ramping would be limited to one inch per hour and for February to mid-June no daylight ramping would be permitted.

Yet a third critical issue was maximum diversions. The agreement set a maximum diversion of 1,000 cfs in the spring for refill purposes—Feb. 15 until the lake was full or until July 1. When the lake was full Cascade could divert 400 cfs to maintain lake levels and provide for eventual municipal water supplies. As fall drawdown began after Sept. 15, only 150 cfs would be diverted. Cascade's water supply needs would be 75 cfs and a peak of 135 cfs, a reduction of 25 percent from the PSE flows. This all meant that leaving more water in the river was possible and workable with municipal water supply needs. All diversions were subject to maintaining the minimum flow in the basin.

A final issue of discussion with the Puyallup Tribe was the amount of release from the tailrace, the outflow from the Powerhouse, which is the

> It was an historic action when the Muckleshoot Indian Tribe, the Puyallup Tribe of Indians and Cascade forged an agreement that all sides agreed provided protection of fish, habitat, municipal water supply and recreation in the White River and Lake Tapps.

only way to release water from Lake Tapps. The minimum had been 50 cfs or as low as Cascade could get it. Once Cascade understood the Lake Tapps system, it was evident it could go much lower. Diversion of 20 cfs was permitted at all times so that the fish screen could operate properly.

By mid-2006 the Muckleshoot Indian Tribe had joined the conversation, focusing on the same four issues, but adding habitat and hatchery capital funding as well. "The negotiations went well," Gagliardo says. "We spent most of our time creating the White River Management Agreement that outlined operational requirements. We had separate agreements with each of the Tribes which included financial settlements and other considerations, and came to agreement in mid-2008 for the joint efforts as well. It took about three years and was a strong statement about cooperation and everyone getting what worked for them." Those financial settlements came with some restrictions primarily that the funds had to be used for environmental enhancement and fish habitat purposes. Each Tribe established special accounts and would develop work plans and budgets for critical habitat and restoration efforts. Gagliardo credited Lloyd Warren's relationship with the Tribes in helping secure the agreement that would help fish and the hatcheries.

It was an historic action when the Muckleshoot Indian Tribe, the Puyallup Tribe of Indians and Cascade forged an agreement that all sides agreed provided protection of fish, habitat, municipal water supply and recreation in the White River and Lake Tapps. More specifically, the White River Management Agreement (WRMA) included a complicated flow regime providing for minimum flows in the White River and for diversions of water from the White River to the Lake Tapps Reservoir. It also has provisions for operation and maintenance of the Lake Tapps system, continued maintenance for recreation lake levels and restoration,

Lloyd Warren of Sammamish Plateau Water and Sewer District and Mary Alyce Burleigh, Kirkland, represented Cascade with representatives from the Muckleshoot and Puyallup Tribes after signing the White River Management Agreement

protection and enhancement of fishery resources and habitat in the White River Basin, funding issues and provisions requiring Tribal support for the Lake Tapps project and water rights. Additionally, the agreements between Cascade and each Tribe provided Cascade security in its anticipated new municipal water rights and provided funding for fishing and natural resource programs including operation for the Muckleshoot Indian Tribe hatchery, habitat restoration and enhancement projects. The final WRMA, signed by both Tribal councils and Cascade in 2008 included the following:

- Flow regimes consisting of a minimum flow to be maintained in the White River;
- Diversion plans for spring refill and fall drawdown, flows, ramping rates and lake elevations;
- Stream flow and lake level monitoring and gauging;
- Water trust providing additional protection for water allocation to increase stream flows;
- Water quality monitoring;
- Establishment of a coordinating committee; and
- Force majeure and dispute resolution.

Cascade and the Muckleshoot agreed to mitigation funds for habitat enhancement/acquisition and hatchery work and support for federal funding of the Corps' fish trap and barrier dam. Cascade paid $6.8 million to the Tribe.

Cascade's agreements with the Puyallups also included support for settlement costs related to the project and support for operations following the final issuance of the municipal water rights. Total cost of this agreement was $14.5 million.

As part of the Tribal settlements, Cascade agreed to include the WRMA provisions in the State Department of Ecology municipal water rights. The thoughtful calculations that had gone into the negotiations ensured the compatibility of a full lake, future water supply and water in streams for fish.

This historic agreement was signed June 26, 2008 at an event with Cascade and the respective Tribal Councils on the Muckleshoot Reservation.

June 26, 2008
historic signing

7.
CASCADE'S NEW NEIGHBORS – THE LAKE TAPPS HOMEOWNERS

The homeowners around Lake Tapps had purchased lovely residences on a lake. They fully expected to have access to that lake for recreational pursuits, and that their property value would continue to grow.

Many residents had been there for decades and several families had relatives living in neighboring homes. So it was gut-wrenching for this close-knit community to follow PSE's decision to sell Lake Tapps to Cascade Water Alliance. Homeowners had worked too hard, they contended, to save their lake to let anything or anyone jeopardize the Lake Tapps Task Force results. Where homeowners had feared and distrusted PSE, they now feared the new, and to them far worse, entity— the unknown Cascade Water Alliance. That made Lake Tapps a wary community at best as Cascade reached out to forge a relationship.

In 2004, PSE had signed an agreement concerning Lake Tapps reservoir management that assured residents would have a lake. Cascade fully assumed this as part of the sale and Pierce County, which had facilitated those discussions, was heavily involved in crafting the agreement. But unsure of Cascade's true intentions, homeowners were insistent that Cascade honor every part of the agreement, even though the operations and Cascade would use the reservoir for were dramatically different from those of PSE.

Central to their uneasiness was that every homeowner's deed dated back to 1954 when PSE sold the land to the Lake Tapps Development

Opposite: Life on Lake Tapps (upper and lower right photos courtesy of Janice Thomas)

Sunrise over Lake Tapps (Photo by Janice Thomas)

Company. Those deeds contained a clause stating that PSE—or its successor—could raise and lower the water within the reservoir at any time and could even "abandon the said storage reservoir at any time at all without any liability for the damage suffered…" That clause terrified the community. They feared all they'd worked for could be in danger and that clause in their deed would override any newer agreement. An initial meeting with the homeowners and Cascade in early 2008 had been a fiasco. Advisors to the homeowners had directed them not to speak to Cascade. Even as Cascade laid out its hopes of being a good neighbor and ensuring Lake Tapps would be preserved, homeowners did not make eye contact with Cascade or speak one word. No further meetings were set.

However, Lake Tapps homeowner attorneys were still greatly involved after the sale of the reservoir, and they sent multiple memos that stipulated demands. Homeowners made it very clear they were not going to let their guard down until they got what they wanted from Cascade, as they had in the 2004 agreement with PSE.

Local homeowners and lakefront residents didn't trust Cascade to protect their interests over future drinking water demands and instream flows on the White River. They viewed Cascade's future municipal water supply and agreements with the Tribes as direct threats to their lake levels. This despite the fact that in purchasing Lake Tapps, Cascade legally assumed PSE's agreements. Yet, because Cascade was not a hydroelectric producer, some modifications of the agreement needed to be made, but Cascade was open to a positive, supportive relationship. Still, the potential changes in the agreement raised a red flag for the Lake Tapps Community Council. Finally homeowners requested a meeting with Cascade and PSE to discuss the agreement Cascade proposed to execute with the Muckleshoot Indian Tribe and the Puyallup Tribe of Indians regarding lake levels.

It didn't help the atmosphere that in March 2008, State Representative Chris Hurst from the 31st District and Pierce County Councilman Shawn Bunney, a Lake Tapps resident with a past involvement regarding water issues, accused Cascade of treating the Lake Tapps community as "nothing more than a necessary annoyance."

Majestic Mount Rainier looms over Lake Tapps

FINALLY STARTING THE CONVERSATION

That was why one of Oberg's first hirings at Cascade in mid-2008 was community relations support to help face hostile opponents. Cascade tried for some time to establish an entrée into the group to assure homeowners it wanted to be a good neighbor and come to agreements on critical issues. It requested a meeting… more than once… but calls and emails to the homeowners group went unanswered.

Cascade contacted everyone in any authority around the lake, from Bonney Lake to Auburn to Sumner and Buckley. Finally, one reply came. Don Morrison, City of Bonney Lake Administrator, agreed to meet. Morrison and his staff met with Cascade and explained the issues, the community concerns and the city's issues—all very reasonable. They too had plans and wanted to know what Cascade had in mind and what kind of neighbor Cascade would be. With the input from Morrison, Lloyd Warren, Cascade's new board chair, requested another visit with the community council. The council's attorney wrote back that a meeting would only be held if Cascade said how it would comply with previous obligations. Finally, after months of letters, Cascade got a letter agreeing to a meeting.

Cascade meets the Lake Tapps community at North Tapps Middle School, 2010

As the meeting began, it was clear that hostility was still very strong. No one spoke for several minutes. Eventually, after what was a painful silence, one member, John Farrell, issued a long list of previous grievances that demonstrated anger, distrust and dislike for and of Cascade. What followed was an even longer period of silence until all Lake Tapps representatives, as one, nodded in agreement.

(Photo by Janice Thomas)

But then something rather extraordinary happened. Shawn Bunney, a Pierce County Council member, spoke up from the back of the room. "Cascade has come to meet with us and offered to work with us." The room was silent as he continued. "We have not been satisfied with what we've heard in the past. This is a new effort and I think the time has come to meet them halfway. Let's tell them our issues and let's listen to what they have to say and see what we can achieve."

It was as if air had been let back into the room. After Bunney's wise words, the members of the community began to talk. The discussion focused primarily on lake levels during the summer. The meeting was short, but was more productive than Cascade staff had experienced in the past, and both sides became cautiously optimistic. A follow up meeting was promised to review lake levels

Back in Bellevue, Cascade's newly hired CEO Chuck Clarke was brought up to speed on where Cascade was with the Lake Tapps community. Although he had not yet started work, Clarke attended the follow up meeting with a few of the leaders of the Lake Tapps Community Council. Also attending were Leon Stucki, Ralph Mason, Ron Wilderman, Ken Castile, and President Chuck Romeo. Clarke later met with Kirk Shuler as well.

"What do you need?" Clarke asked.

"A full lake all summer long," was the unanimous response.

"Well, I think we can make that happen even with the agreement for instream flows and the eventual use of water supply," Clarke said.

After so much silence and anger, it seemed a real conversation was beginning. The community council representatives were pleased, but skeptical. Many of them had been engineers during their careers at Boeing and Weyerhaeuser and had spent the last several years gathering

Clarke knew gaining the trust of the community was a critical outcome for Cascade. After the work with the four retired engineers, word filtered to the other community council members that Cascade was willing to come to the table and listen. It may have happened slowly with just a handful of residents, but the mood was shifting.

information from a variety of sources. They had created their own models of the lake operations, flows and all aspects of the project. Ken Castile's wife, Carol, said her husband had an entire room filled with boxes of his studies and his work on this topic. The Lake Tapps retired engineers told Cascade that the numbers they had said it couldn't be done. But they were also intrigued to see how the new Cascade CEO said it could and they agreed to bring their work to the table to find out how. And, there was something else that made things look up—Chuck Clarke even being at that meeting. "I'll never forget how that impressed us," Stucki said. "He hadn't even started the job. That was the beginning of turning things around for us."

Clarke brought in Owen Reese of Aspect Engineering to work with the Lake Tapps team. Reese had a contract in place with the State Department of Ecology for water rights modeling. The four Lake Tapps engineers came to the meeting, computers and modeling in hand. Ken Castile brought the slide rule he had used at the very beginning of the Lake Tapps Task Force discussions.

Chuck Clarke began the first meeting with a commitment to getting full understanding, transparency, and a workable solution. Owen Reese came, armed with his data and modeling. The engineers and Reese spent several four-hour meetings at the Tapps Island Clubhouse. He showed them all his data and information. The engineers shared with him their data, figures, assumptions and expectations.

The modeling was surprisingly close. But Reese had more up-to-date and accurate numbers and information that he shared. He showed the others where their numbers, while very close, needed to be updated and why. Mutual respect grew between Reese and the Lake Tapps group. Even the most skeptical participant, Castile, finally agreed that it seemed possible that the homeowners could get the lake levels they wanted. The instream flows could still be respected and Cascade could, eventually, use the lake for municipal water supply. It was a pivotal moment.

(Photo by Janice Thomas)

Lake Tapps Community Council President Chuck Romeo said that "after a rocky start we all really hit it off. Chuck Clarke knew what we needed. He said we can all get what we want, and he was really very realistic. That was the key to us and to the community and Cascade getting together."

Clarke knew gaining the trust of the community was a critical outcome for Cascade. After the work with the four retired engineers, word filtered to the other community council members that Cascade was willing to come to the table and listen. It may have happened slowly with just a handful of residents, but the mood was shifting.

REACHING AN AGREEMENT

About 60 hours' worth of subsequent meetings were held with the Lake Tapps Community Council, representing the homeowners' associations around the lake. The Lake Tapps homeowners' attorney Liz Thomas of K&L Gates and Cascade's T.C. Richmond of VanNess Feldman put in several late nights on the many versions of draft agreements—which were actually quite similar to those from the PSE agreement for basic lake related obligations. Drafts were circulated among staff and residents. All stakeholders had their say and it seemed that finally, an agreement was reached. The agreement included the following:

- Cascade will maintain normal full recreational levels (between elevation 541.5 and 543 feet) from April 15 through Sept. 30 for 30 years or until use of Lake Tapps for municipal water supply starts, whichever is later;

- Cascade will make all reasonable efforts to maintain that normal full pool through Oct. 31;
- Both parties will have a lake management team to review annual operations of the reservoir, such as spring refill and fall drawdown; and
- Either Cascade or the homeowners can propose modifications to the agreement.

In addition, a very broad adaptive management language was prepared and agreed upon.

Signed agreement with the homeowners

IN WITNESS WHEREOF, the parties have executed this Agreement as of the date first above written.

Chuck Clarke, CEO
Cascade Water Alliance

Charles Romeo, President
Lake Tapps Community Council

Leon Stucki, Snag Island Maintenance Association;
VP & Director, Lake Tapps Community Council

James Diebag, GM Tapps Island Association;
Director, Lake Tapps Community Council

John Farrell, Church Lake Maintenance Co;
Director, Lake Tapps Community Council

Vickie Karuzas, Inlet Island Maintenance Co;
Director, Lake Tapps Community Council

Cliff McIntosh, President
West Tapps Maintenance Co

Tacoma Point Improvement Club

Joseph Muscarnera, President
Driftwood Point Association

Ralph Mason, Director At Large
Lake Tapps Community Council

Kirk Shuler, Director At Large
Lake Tapps Community Council

Ron Wilderman, Director
Lake Tapps Community Council

Don Fisher, Treasurer
Lake Tapps Community Council

Michelle Whittmier, Director
Lake Tapps Community Council

From adversaries to partners, compromise was reached. More importantly, relationships were developed and trust was gained on both sides. Finally, after ten years of discussions and Cascade's extensive outreach, the homeowners and the new lake owners came to an agreement about the future of Lake Tapps. The Lake Tapps

> "As the future owners of this beautiful natural resource, we want to assure the community we are here to be a good neighbor now and in the future. We are proud of this agreement and proud to call the Lake Tapps community a partner."

Community agreement would protect the recreational levels of the lake and give Cascade, and perhaps eventually the region, an ongoing drinking water resource. And so, on Friday, April 10, 2009, the documents were officially signed in a champagne ceremony at the Tapps Island Clubhouse, where so many of the initial meetings had taken place.

Cascade's Chair Lloyd Warren told community members that, "As the future owners of this beautiful natural resource, we want to assure the community we are here to be a good neighbor now and in the future. We are proud of this agreement and proud to call the Lake Tapps community a partner."

Lake Tapps Community Council Chair Chuck Romeo added, "I bought my lot in 1965 and built my house in 1966. I raised my family on Lake Tapps and my daughter lives next to me today. This is a great and very tight knit community and I couldn't imagine what it would be like

Chuck Romeo, Lake Tapps, seated left, and Chuck Clarke, Cascade, seated right

Spreading the news

without the lake here—it would be a great loss. I give a lot of credit to Cascade and am very pleased to know that this agreement provides an ongoing legacy for my kids, grandkids and this community into the future." Even the local press made note of this significant event. Dennis Box of the *Bonney Lake and Sumner Courier Herald* wrote:

"The memorandum potentially brings to a close 10 years of anxiety, anger and potential litigation over the future survival of the reservoir." (April 19, 2009.)

The News Tribune opined "Boaters and fisherman, rejoice. A deal in the offing could help ensure that your beloved Lake Tapps will be around for decades to come." (April 14, 2009.)

The Seattle Times reported that "Years of stormy negotiations about the future dual use of Lake Tapps as a municipal water supply and recreational amenity have been successfully resolved….this agreement… is good news for fish, cities and recreation." (April 22, 2009)

The effort was so well received that a community fundraiser was held at the Bonney Lake restaurant Al Lago to complete the work of the "Lake Savers," sponsored by Cascade Water Alliance.

Ralph Mason, Lake Tapps, and Elaine Kraft, Cascade; and Lloyd and Rosemary Warren and Michael Gagliardo of Cascade

ONGOING CONNECTION

Once the agreement was signed, Cascade wanted to meet with the Lake Tapps community as a whole. To introduce itself, Cascade held a "come meet us" event at North Tapps Middle School on Feb 10, 2010. Cascade wasn't sure yet of the best way to reach homeowners in the Lake Tapps area so an extensive outreach was used, including postcards, emails, homeowner association news, the Lake Tapps News (run by the always-on-the-spot Sue Brentson) and the Bonney Lake Courier Herald.

Cascade brought all its staff and prepared technical materials on Cascade's plan for eventual water supply. Board members and elected officials came as well. The tone of the meeting was one of welcome with coffee and cookies ready for all attendees. The staff stood by to greet the new neighbors… if anyone came to the 6 p.m. meeting. By 5:30, crowds began coming in earnest. Cascade staff and board members tried valiantly to keep up with the Lake Tapps homeowners, greeting them and getting their contact information so Cascade could follow up with future communications. All in all, about 150 folks crammed into the Middle School cafeteria, wanting to see who owned their lake and what the plans were for it. The cookies went fast, and the meeting faster.

Cascade's goal of letting the community know who it was, introducing its staff and how they could be reached was met with dozens of questions about the future of the lake. Cascade outlined its plans for eventual use of the reservoir for municipal drinking water, but assured residents they'd have their lake full in the summer, barring a lack of rain or other emergency issues. And, for the first time in recent history, Lake Tapps Community

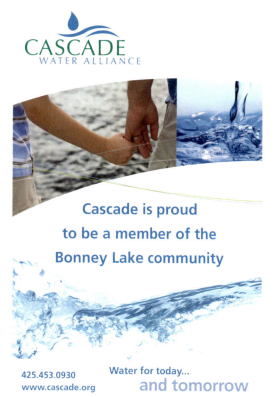

Cascade ad

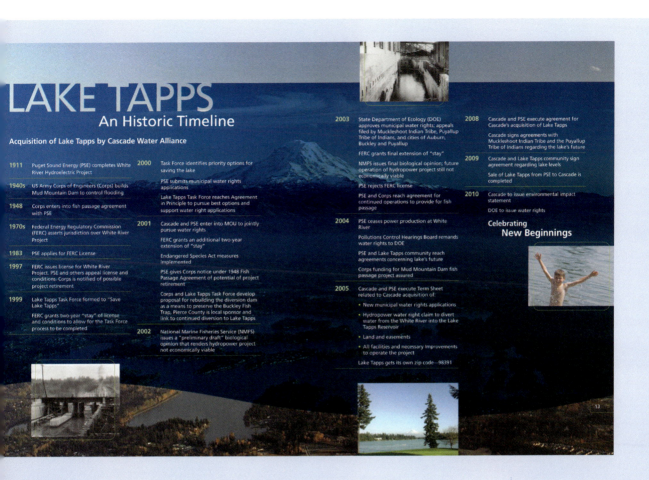

LAKE TAPPS
An Historic Timeline

Acquisition of Lake Tapps by Cascade Water Alliance

1911	Puget Sound Energy (PSE) completes White River Hydroelectric Project
1940s	US Army Corps of Engineers (Corps) builds Mud Mountain Dam to control flooding
1948	Corps enters into fish passage agreement with PSE
1970s	Federal Energy Regulatory Commission (FERC) asserts jurisdiction over White River Project
1983	PSE applies for FERC License
1997	FERC issues license for White River Project. PSE and others appeal license and conditions. Corps is notified of possible project retirement
1999	Lake Tapps Task Force formed to "Save Lake Tapps" FERC grants two-year "stay" of license and conditions to allow for the Task Force process to be completed
2000	Task Force identifies priority options for saving the lake PSE submits municipal water rights applications Lake Tapps Task Force reaches Agreement in Principle to pursue best options and support water right applications
2001	Cascade and PSE enter into MOU to jointly pursue water rights FERC grants an additional two-year extension of "stay" Endangered Species Act measures Implemented PSE gives Corps notice under 1948 Fish Passage Agreement of potential of project retirement Corps and Lake Tapps Task Force develop proposal for rebuilding the diversion dam as a means to preserve the Buckley Fish Trap. Pierce County is local sponsor and link to continued diversion to Lake Tapps
2002	National Marine Fisheries Service (NMFS) issues a "preliminary draft" biological opinion that renders hydropower project not economically viable
2003	State Department of Ecology (DOE) approves municipal water rights; appeals filed by Muckleshoot Indian Tribe, Puyallup Tribe of Indians, and cities of Auburn, Buckley and Puyallup FERC grants final extension of "stay" NMFS issues final biological opinion; future operation of hydropower project still not economically viable PSE rejects FERC license PSE and Corps reach agreement for continued operations to provide for fish passage
2004	PSE ceases power production at White River Pollutions Control Hearings Board remands water rights to DOE PSE and Lake Tapps community reach agreements concerning lake's future Corps funding for Mud Mountain Dam fish passage project assured
2005	Cascade and PSE execute Term Sheet related to Cascade acquisition of: • New municipal water rights applications • Hydropower water right claim to divert water from the White River into the Lake Tapps Reservoir • Land and easements • All facilities and necessary improvements to operate the project Lake Tapps gets its own zip code—98391
2008	Cascade and PSE execute agreement for Cascade's acquisition of Lake Tapps Cascade signs agreements with Muckleshoot Indian Tribe and the Puyallup Tribe of Indians regarding the lake's future
2009	Cascade and Lake Tapps community sign agreement regarding lake levels Sale of Lake Tapps from PSE to Cascade is completed
2010	Cascade to issue environmental impact statement DOE to issue water rights

Celebrating New Beginnings

Lake Tapps | It's Our Lake
planning together for tomorrow

swim safe

Know Lake Tapps
It's from a glacier

It's really cold – 55 degrees! Your body loses heat 30 times faster in water

The colder the water the quicker cold water incapacitation will occur

- Everyone's at risk, especially the elderly, children, people with lower body fat
- Males (whose bodies generally cool faster than females) are at greater risk
- An average adult has a 50% chance of surviving a 50 yard swim in 50 degree water

Know your limits
Drownings happen when you

- Are too cold
- Are too tired
- Are too far from safety
- Have had too much sun
- Have had too much strenuous activity
- Don't know how to swim well
- Use alcohol or drugs
- Don't wear a life jacket

Know how to protect yourself and your loved ones
Weather and water conditions change quickly. No matter how good a swimmer you are, the water can overpower your skills. Swim safe!

- Wear a life jacket when boating, tubing, and rafting
- Wear a life jacket when swimming where there are no lifeguards
- Watch for shivering, altered judgment, blue fingers, toes or lips
- Learn how to swim
- Learn CPR
- Know what to do when in trouble

In an emergency
Do not hesitate, immediately call **911**

Lake Tapps photo by Janice Thomas.

Sponsored by

Council members stood with Cascade and urged others to consider them good neighbors.

To continue developing this relationship, Cascade's outreach includes annual meetings, as well as special meetings that have focused on milfoil, a Lake Tapps Management Policy, and collaborative efforts with area communities to ensure everyone is aware of how cold that lake is. This recent coordinated, community wide SwimSafe campaign has created an environment of awareness where, as of this writing, three summers have passed without a drowning death.

Cascade also hosts events and activities in the Lake Tapps area, is an active member of the Bonney Lake Chamber. With the help of the Courier Heralds' Dottie Bergstresser, Cascade became a frequent advertiser and a constant presence in the Herald and Auburn Reporter, sharing news with the community. Each year a new "Who to Call" information sheet is updated, letting residents know who to call for which services around Lake Tapps. It is printed in the Bonney Lake Courier Herald around Memorial Day and posted on both Cascade's and the Lake Tapps website. While Cascade and the homeowners agreed to meet formally twice a year to discuss spring fill and fall drawdown of lake levels, the Cascade staff and various Lake Tapps leaders meet and talk much more frequently.

(Photo on right courtesy of Janice Thomas)

Leon Stucki said that for "a public organization, I haven't seen one that works as streamlined efficient and successful as Cascade." Ken Castile adds that "I'm glad now Cascade bought the lake. I was never sure we could have paid for the whole thing or what else we might have done." Ralph Mason adds that "we couldn't have done better," and Chuck Romeo said "if there's a question of who we'd rather have—PSE or Cascade—there's no question."

The tone and attitude around the lake has evolved into a positive partnership, with residents now confident in their relationship with Cascade. Leon Stucki said that for "a public organization, I haven't seen one that works as streamlined efficient and successful as Cascade." Ken Castile adds that "I'm glad now Cascade bought the lake. I was never sure we could have paid for the whole thing or what else we might have done." Ralph Mason adds that "we couldn't have done better," and Chuck Romeo said "if there's a question of who we'd rather have—PSE or Cascade—there's no question."

A decade long struggle gave way to a stable future for Lake Tapps and outstanding working relationships with Cascade Water Alliance.

8.
CASCADE'S NEW NEIGHBORS—THE FOUR CITIES

Surrounding Lake Tapps are four cities—Auburn, Bonney Lake, Buckley and Sumner—that were no strangers to the concern for water supply.

Auburn Mayor Pete Lewis

About the time Cascade and Puget Sound Energy were in discussions for a joint water rights application, Auburn was undertaking a major multi-million-dollar study regarding the aquifer that ran off Mount Rainier, through Auburn and pooled beneath the city's geographical boundaries. Just as they finished the study, former Auburn Mayor Pete Lewis recalled, "We got word that the State Department of Ecology had closed our basin. Auburn was going to be required to build out for more growth, but couldn't take any more water from its ground wells to support that growth."

Lewis and his fellow mayors in the Lake Tapps area, who had been part of the Lake Tapps Task Force, began to grow concerned as the efforts by PSE and Cascade seemed to solidify. The cities knew they needed more water and decided they would try and get a water right. As they surrounded the lake, the move seemed to make good sense. But PSE had already filed for the water right to use the water, which meant PSE was in line ahead of the cities.

"That just united us. We were all facing the same problem—enough water for our residents," Lewis said. So, the four mayors formed a coalition and formally joined together to take action. While the Tribes and the homeowners had been wary of Cascade, the cities actually wanted to stop Cascade altogether.

The coalition met with the State Department of Ecology to discuss next steps. The cities' history with the Lake Tapps Task Force meant they were familiar with the process and the issues facing them. Still, they were surprised when they heard that Cascade and Puget Sound Energy had reached a deal for Cascade to purchase the entire White River/Lake Tapps system rather than just share water rights. The cities' concerns grew more serious and put some members of the coalition in a unique position. Mayor Lewis, and Sumner Mayor Dave Enslow in particular, worked with the mayors and elected officials who sat on Cascade's board (Degginger, Marchione, Haggerton, Fred Butler and others) on several other regional projects yet opposed them on Lake Tapps.

Sumner Mayor Dave Enslow

"I'd go to meetings of the Puget Sound Regional Council or Suburban Cities and we'd all be working together on regional issues," said Lewis. "Mayor Enslow would go to Sound Transit and work on regional transportation issues with these same individuals we were now fighting. We got along fine and would all work together on other issues, but on water and in particular Lake Tapps, we were very far apart, and definitely on opposite sides of the table. It was very difficult."

The major concern the four cities shared was that if Cascade used the lake for municipal water supply, and had to draw the lake down to do so, their cities might face a significant impact on their wells and water supply. Their concerns became public knowledge when a newspaper article quoted Mayor Lewis stating "there was no way our water was going to Bellevue," and that he was going to fight to keep Lake Tapps water in his community for his residents.

MEETING HIT AND MISS

As the mayor of the largest of the four cities, Lewis became the group's de facto leader. "It was hard," Lewis said. "Both sides dug our heels in. We were all fairly opinionated." It didn't help that when the cities first agreed to meet with Cascade leaders to discuss the situation the meeting was, they all concurred, a disaster. There was a series of miscommunications that left both sides feeling disrespected. Both Lewis

Working Together to Benefit the Region

Despite all the rain we get in our region, a supply of clean, safe water remains a most precious commodity. Making sure we have it in the future means planning for it today.

Looking to that future, we as regional partners worked together towards a solution. The cities of Auburn, Bonney Lake, Buckley and Sumner guaranteed they **will** have water to meet the needs of our communities. Working with the Cascade Water Alliance, the new owner of Lake Tapps, a solution has been reached that is a win for everyone – and water for us all.

Just a few years ago, there was considerable doubt about the future of Lake Tapps. Puget Sound Energy was halting hydroelectric production and there was a possibility that the lake would literally dry up. But concerned citizens rallied and formed the Lake Tapps Task Force to find a way to save the lake for future generations. Using the lake as a drinking water supply was a potential solution.

At this same time, the Cascade Water Alliance was being formed. Its members were looking for new municipal water supplies which would meet the growing needs of the region. Cascade became an enthusiastic party in the Lake Tapps negotiations. But could a solution meeting Cascade's future needs work for Auburn, Bonney Lake, Buckley and Sumner too?

What looked like an intractable situation – a stalemate on all sides – has now been resolved. Concerned leaders, two Tribes, local communities, and homeowners around Lake Tapps sat down with Cascade and hammered out agreements ensuring everyone's needs would be met from the Lake Tapps system and local water sources. Water – for people, for fish and for recreation.

As leaders, we can tell you; this was not an easy process. It was a protracted series of tough negotiations. But we can also tell you it is regional leadership at its best. We are proud of the results of our efforts to make sure Lake Tapps remains the wonderful regional jewel it is while we provide water for decades to come for all of our citizens. Cascade is a welcome part of this community.

Auburn Mayor Pete Lewis and Lloyd Warren, Chair, Cascade Water Alliance Board of Directors

Pete Lewis, Mayor, City of Auburn (left)
Lloyd Warren, Chair, Cascade Water Alliance (right)

February 5, 2010

and Cascade board member Degginger agreed it was "an interesting time." And, while future meetings were attempted, no common ground could be found.

But in 2009, as the sale of Lake Tapps to Cascade was getting close, the entities tried again. The finality of the sale and different Cascade staff brought a new willingness to consider future talks. Once they reconvened, it was with the help of outside parties who were known and respected by all. This time the talks began at the staff level. Tim Thompson, who had worked for then Congressman Norm Dicks, was now with Thompson Smitch Consulting. He and Jim Waldo a well-known water and government attorney who had the trust of all members at the table, began discussions.

Both sides came to the table very cautiously, willing to put aside past dealings. Representatives from Cascade, Auburn's Dennis Dowdy and Caroline Robertson, Bonney Lake's Dan Grigsby, Buckley's Dave Schmidt, Sumner's Diane Supler and Bill Pugh met with several attorneys, including Tom Pors, VanNess Feldman's TC Richmond and Adam Gravley. Much like the discussions with the homeowners, the four cities' discussions began with Cascade's Chuck Clarke wisely asking each city what it needed. The four cities agreed to come up with their actual needs and exact water demands. This took a couple of months.

THE QUEST FOR EMINENT DOMAIN

Meanwhile, Cascade was at the Legislature trying to obtain the right of eminent domain, something not originally granted with the Interlocal state statute under which Cascade had been created. Cascade was not a utility or a government, so it did not have this basic authority so essential for its future operations. An eclectic group of Cascade's representatives, business leaders and developers from East King County worked together on a fix. They all knew the Eastside could only grow if it had water…and that Cascade was the best entity to secure that supply. Working together to pass the legislation made sense for everyone.

Mayor Lewis realized this created an ideal opportunity for the cities. "I saw an opportunity to get Cascade to the table and keep them there

> "I saw an opportunity to get Cascade to the table and keep them there while our negotiations were underway," Lewis said. "We would not allow any Cascade pipeline coming through our city borders unless we could be assured of water for the future. I wanted to strike while the iron was hot."

Eminent domain authority is assured—with some caveats! Cascade's Elaine Kraft, left, and Grant Degginger, Bellevue Mayor, right. Gordon Thomas Honeywell President Tim Schellberg, middle, lobbyist for Cascade, watch as Gov. Chris Gregoire signs the bill into law

while our negotiations were underway," Lewis said. "We would not allow any Cascade pipeline coming through our city borders unless we could be assured of water for the future. I wanted to strike while the iron was hot." The message was clear. If Cascade couldn't work with Auburn for its future water needs, there would be no eminent domain nor any Cascade pipe finding its way to the Eastside through the City of Auburn.

As the days of the legislative session wound down to adjournment, an agreement was struck to add some conditional language to the bill. It

Signing the agreement are Mayor Dave Enslow, Sumner, Chuck Clarke, Cascade, and Mayor Pete Lewis, right. Not pictured are Pat Johnson, Buckley mayor or Neil Johnson, Bonney Lake mayor.

would require Cascade to ensure water supply was available for the four cities' future needs before eminent domain could be used within their borders. "We needed leverage to keep them at the table. If we could get a deal, we'd get rid of that restrictive language in the bill later," said Lewis.

For Cascade, the language in the bill would make routing and siting a pipeline very difficult and far costlier, but it was willing to allow the restrictive language to remain in the bill to get the eminent domain provision. Cascade was confident that the talks were proceeding well. The gauntlet thrown, the eminent domain legislation passed with the Auburn language in the bill.

BACK FROM THE DRAWING BOARD

The cities came back to the table with their specific needs and water requirements. Auburn needed water supply. Buckley was worried about its groundwater supplies. Geographically, Sumner was in a different location and needed water from the Lake Tapps tailrace. Bonney Lake was on the shores of a lake that Cascade now owned. With this feedback, Cascade staff believed that the same data and modeling used with the Lake Tapps homeowners clearly indicated that even if there was drawdown for water supply it would not affect the four cities' supply and that Cascade could provide the water each of the four cities needed in the future. Still, it took weeks of discussions to figure out the details of how to meet the needs of the four cities. Meetings were held in Tim Thompson's offices off Rustin Way on Tacoma's waterfront, a neutral and beautiful location appropriately overlooking Puget Sound waters.

Finally in late January 2010, after months of working together in the spirit of regional partnership, the cities of Auburn, Bonney Lake, Buckley and Sumner came to an innovative and unique agreement with Cascade. In its soon to be submitted water right, Cascade would assure that 10 cfs would be left in the White River should the cities need it. The deal would guarantee the four cities sufficient water to help them meet their water needs over the next 50 years.

Under the terms of the plan, called the Lake Tapps Water Resources Agreement (LTWRA,) Cascade would assist each of the four cities individually and collectively to meet its future water supply needs. Additionally, the agreement required Cascade leave the 10 cfs of water in the White River that would be available to mitigate ground water withdrawals if and when the cities applied for a water right from the State Department of Ecology. The four cities further agreed to support Cascade's water right and that the provisions of this agreement for mitigation water would be included and codified in the water right.

But the most critical element was the option for development of wholesale contracts between the four cities and Cascade to transfer water Cascade had purchased from the City of Tacoma to the cities, at a discounted price. Cascade would still have to meet permit requirements and franchises when operating within the four cities. Elected officials from Cascade and the four cities came together to support the agreements that solidified Cascade's commitment to resolve any impacts its Lake Tapps operations might have on any of the four cities' current water supply.

One final element of the agreement enabled removing the limiting language the four cities had added to the Cascade eminent domain legislation in 2009. In February, 2010, when the agreement between Cascade and the four cities was finalized, the four cities agreed to allow the onerous language once attached to Cascade's eminent domain legislation to be removed, and the new legislation was signed into law shortly after.

Just one year later, following the agreement with the four cities, restrictive language is removed and Cascade has its eminent domain authority. Degginger, Kraft and bill sponsor State Senator Pam Roach of Auburn, left, and Megan Schrader, Gordon Thomas Honeywell and bill sponsor State Rep. Roger Goodman, of Kirkland, right watch Gov. Chris Gregoire sign the new bill into law.

9.
PUTTING ALL THE PIECES TOGETHER

What Cascade had accomplished was nothing short of amazing. It had finalized agreements with PSE, the Tribes, the homeowners and the four cities surrounding Lake Tapps.

Now, for Cascade to be able to eventually use Lake Tapps for municipal water supply it needed a state issued water right. Finalizing that was critical. The support, or at least neutrality, among involved parties needed to support moving forward for a water right.

Under Washington State law, the state's waters collectively belong to the public and cannot be owned by any one individual or group. Instead, individuals or groups may be granted rights, or legal authorization, to use a predefined quantity of public water for a designated purpose. This purpose must qualify as a beneficial, non-wasteful use such as irrigation, domestic water supply or power generation. State law requires any use of surface water (lakes, ponds, rivers, streams, or springs) which began after the state water code was enacted in 1917 to have a water-right permit or certificate.

The pathway to Lake Taps water rights originally began when PSE and Cascade sought to obtain the in 2001 from the Department of Ecology. The effort was unsuccessful. But now that Cascade would be using the reservoir for water supply. Ecology staff and consultants had already done complicated technical analyses when examining water rights in 2005.

Then in February 2008, when Cascade's board of directors finally approved the purchase of Lake Tapps they accepted PSE's ongoing three

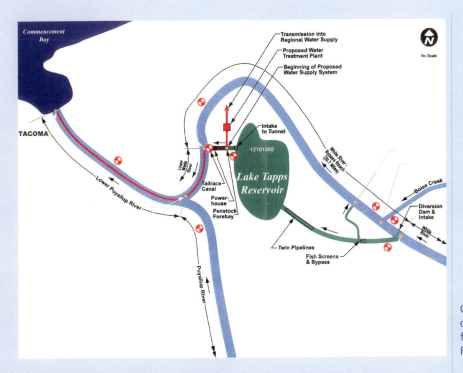

Graphic description of the flow of the White River system

municipal water rights applications, a pre-code water right claim and the change/transfer applications (S2-29920, R2-29935 and S2-29934). As the sale became final at the end of 2009, Cascade became the owner of the entire project.

By this time Jay Manning, then the director of the State Department of Ecology, and his staff had been working with all the parties involved in the Lake Tapps issues for some time. It had been complicated, difficult and at times problematic.

In fact, the process and issues had gotten considerably more complicated than they needed to be. But now, as each side sized up the new people at the table, each gave some ground where it could. In the end, Manning, said, the new relationships and agreements changed the entire dynamic. Cascade and consultants worked diligently with Ecology

> "We worked as partners. We forged a good team and got a good outcome. It was unique as water rights go—we went from power generating water rights to municipal water supply and recreational levels, but our positive partnership got us there."

Environmental leader Jay Manning

to combine all elements of the recent agreements with the Tribes, the homeowners and the four cities into the water right, codifying the results of these complicated negotiations into water right permit conditions and a workable solution. Together they took a situation that had been frustrating, and very time consuming for a thinly stretched Ecology staff, and turned it around to get an outcome that was positive for every group, for the environment and for water supply. Cascade was given a 50-year water right development period while most are 20 years or less. But this one could be reexamined if there were issues and that made all parties more amenable.

While Manning said Cascade, Ecology and PSE had an outstanding and collaborative working relationship, there had been a stalemate with the homeowners and four cities until Chuck Clarke arrived in 2009. Manning said, "Chuck has seen it all. Clarke went in to meetings with the homeowners with inclusiveness, respect and transparency. He heard and acknowledged the homeowners' concerns. He was willing to give ground on some issues that hadn't been offered before, and he created a bond of trust with the homeowners. They in turn gave some concessions as well.

"Chuck is very skilled," said Manning. "We worked as partners. We forged a good team and got a good outcome. It was unique as water rights go—we went from power generating water rights to municipal water supply and recreational levels, but our positive partnership got us there. We appreciated Cascade's positive creativity and strategy in reaching consensus," said Manning. "You don't see something like this very often."

Cascade officially requested approval by the Department of Ecology in January 2009 to operate the project for municipal water supply. The three basic elements of the project operation are:

- Divert 54,300 acre feet for municipal purposes and operations consistent with the Water Resources Management Agreement (Tribes) and Homeowners Agreement (S2-29920A;)
- Regional reserved water for the four cities (S2-29920B;)
- Store diverted municipal water in the Lake Tapps Reservoir (R2-29935;)
- Use diverted/stored water for municipal purposes (S2-29934; and
- Claim with added purposes for recreation, fish enhancement, etc. (Claim 160822)

The request sought an annual quantity of the original amount PSE had requested (72,400 acre feet) reduced to 54,300 acre feet. A Draft Environmental Impact Statement (DEIS) was developed and issued. A public comment period was open for about three months and in that

Cascade's board members, joined by Tom Lorranger, left of Ecology, celebrate completion of the water rights. From left, Cascade's Jon Ault, Grant Degginger (holding certificate,) David Knight, Lloyd Warren, John Marchione, Penny Sweet and John Traeger.

Cascade called this the final piece of the puzzle coming together to complete the picture of regional collaboration with partners around Lake Tapps—the Muckleshoot Indian Tribe, the Puyallup Tribe of Indians, the Lake Tapps homeowners and the four cities surrounding the lake, Auburn, Bonney Lake, Buckley and Sumner.

time Cascade received only nine written comments, none of which constituted issues or significant concerns. After considering this input, in June 2010, Cascade approved the actions listed in the water rights and asked Ecology to officially approve the water rights.

Ecology issued a Report of Examination (ROE) approving the use of Lake Tapps as a municipal water supply on Sept. 15, 2010. Final water right permits were issued Dec. 10, 2010.

ONE MORE PIECE TO THE PUZZLE

On Feb. 28, 2014 Cascade issued an addendum to the Final EIS for the Lake Tapps Reservoir Water Rights and Supply Project (June 16, 2010) that included a proposed trust water donation. On Jan. 17, 2015, Cascade Water Alliance made a permanent donation of 684,571 acre feet of water to the state's Trust Water Rights Program. The donation will preserve instream flows and protect fish habitat in a stretch of the White River that flows through the Muckleshoot Indian Reservation. That transaction completed the water right condition from the 2010 Water Resources Management Agreement to donate a portion of the water rights it acquired in the purchase of Lake Tapps to the trust water program. In addition, Cascade donated another 154,751 acre feet of water to the Temporary Trust water rights program until 2034.

The water trust donation keeps water in the river for the benefit of fish, wildlife and the natural environment and does not impact levels of the Lake Tapps reservoir or affect instream flows. The water is still Cascade's, it's just donated to the state for a specific purpose and is not available to appropriate for other water use. This was done to support the Department of Ecology's earlier decision that it would not approve or issue new water rights for 20.7 miles of the White River in what is known as the Reservation Reach between Buckley and Sumner. Several salmon species use this stretch of the river for migration, spawning, rearing and flood refuge.

This donation is the culmination of the water rights package that has converted Lake Tapps in Pierce County into a future municipal water supply for 50 years or longer for Cascade Water Alliance and its members. Ecology Director Maia Bellon said, "Big things happen when the state, local governments and Tribes come together to form strategic partnerships. This historic donation protects water levels for fish, guarantees water supplies for people, and preserves Lake Tapps as a vital community asset for decades to come."

Cascade called this the final piece of the puzzle coming together to complete the picture of regional collaboration with partners around Lake Tapps—the Muckleshoot Indian Tribe, the Puyallup Tribe of Indians, the Lake Tapps homeowners and the four cities surrounding the lake, Auburn, Bonney Lake, Buckley and Sumner. The collective work made possible a municipal water supply for the future, instream flows for fish and a summer recreational reservoir.

Grant Degginger, Cascade board chair and Bellevue mayor, acknowledged that what Cascade had done with its engagement of the public and key agencies had been a success. "I know this," he noted, "because even during these difficult challenges, we didn't hear a single word against Cascade or the need for water. That is because we did our outreach, built coalitions and were transparent. We worked together. We did our work well."

10.
CELEBRATING NEW BEGINNINGS

Sometimes, when everything comes together, you just have to celebrate. And when a milestone is hit right out of the park, you have to celebrate big!

In May 2009, on its 10th anniversary, Cascade hosted a luncheon for 200 partners, marking its first decade of existence. Held at the Museum of Flight in Tukwila, the event feted Cascade's accomplishments, members and those with whom they had worked. Dreams had been envisioned—plans had been made—and major successes had been achieved for this new entity in ensuring the availability of clean, safe and reliable water for its members. These were things it could not have done alone. So, Cascade honored Seattle and Tacoma, PSE, the Tribes and the Lake Tapps Community Council for being partners in making Cascade's first decade successful, including:

- Purchase of Lake Tapps from PSE as the region's first new water supply source in decades;
- Historic agreements with the Muckleshoot Indian Tribe and Puyallup Tribe of Indians that provided for the protection of fish, habitat and stream flows in the White River;
- Agreements with the Lake Tapps community to preserve Lake Tapps as a valuable recreational resource while Cascade develops water supply;
- Renegotiated contracts for water from Seattle and Tacoma; and
- Wise water use programs that save millions of gallons of water per year.

Opposite: Cascade, its friends and partners celebrating 10 years as an organization

By February 2010, agreements were now in place with all the Lake Tapps partners. Cascade decided that those 2010 major milestones surrounding the purchase of Lake Tapps and the agreements with the Tribes, homeowners and four cities called for an even bigger celebration. Out of respect for tradition, and honoring valued partnerships, Cascade took a page from the Lake Tapps Task Force's long history of celebrating successes with a "cake ceremony." Cascade wanted to celebrate its triumvirate of signed agreements with a thank you to the Lake Tapps community. It also wanted to use this event to acknowledge and convey to the region that cooperation and collaboration really do work. The ideal way to commemorate the occasion seemed obvious...by concluding the process the way the Lake Tapps Task Force began.

Gov. Gregoire declares Feb. 5, 2010 as Celebrating New Beginnings Day

Rhonda Hilyer and Cascade's Lloyd Warren

HOMAGE TO THE PROCESS

Cascade immediately contacted Rhonda Hilyer, the facilitator who had helped the Lake Tapps community, about the best way to make this happen. The answer was an easy one—host one final meeting of the Lake Tapps Task Force. They would reconvene to rap the gavel one last time on the efforts to save Lake Tapps—because they had accomplished their ultimate goal.

Hilyer gathered the old materials from the Task Force as she and Cascade staff replicated the time-honored traditions of that group. Each person at the table had his or her respective seat and name tag and they would follow the same established roles and procedures for this meeting. The group would formally end the process of the Lake Tapps Task Force work.

Cascade declared the event "Celebrating New Beginnings" and scheduled it for Feb. 5, 2010. In its powerhouse parking lot on the East Valley Highway, Cascade erected a huge tent—large enough to hold the big square of tables that represented the Lake Tapps Task Force and its more than 40 participants. Pictures and memorabilia from the process were posted around the massive space. Each participant's original name tent card was placed on the table at their respective seat just as they had been at each Task Force meeting.

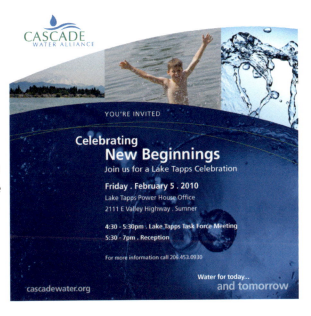

All elected officials who had been a part of the process, as well as newly elected representatives, were invited. Newspapers heralded the tremendous accomplishments being celebrated that day—historic signings with Tribes, homeowners and cities surrounding Lake Tapps. Gov. Chris Gregoire proclaimed Feb. 5, 2010 as "Lake Tapps Celebrating New Beginnings Day." But this was more than just a celebration—it was truly the beginning of a new era of collaboration and cooperation in which every interest won. And to top off the event, as was the tradition of the Task Force, there was cake—the ultimate cake ceremony—indicating the final success.

Hilyer gaveled the final meeting of the Lake Tapps Task Force to order. Former Task Force chairs, Jan Shabro (former Pierce County Councilmember) and John Ladenburg (former Pierce County Executive) officially opened the meeting as they had done for years during the group's work. They handed the gavel to former Pierce County Councilmember Shawn Bunney who regaled the group with his historic perspective and tales of the roller coaster ride of emotions from the first mention of the sale of the lake by PSE to the agreements before the community on that day. Current Pierce County Executive Pat McCarthy

Opposite:
Celebrating
new beginnings
together

"In 1980, a number of us got together to begin a decade-long dialogue about water—about protecting our future and creating our destiny. That discussion became Cascade. Now, 30 years later, we all stand here together, as neighbors, as a community, as partners. Our strength is a shared vision of water for today and tomorrow."

hailed the agreements as "the way things should work" amid applause from the attendees.

Every member of the Task Force spoke, sharing memories—the good, the bad, the fears and the tears. Participants no longer alive were recalled fondly, including the late Congresswoman Jennifer Dunn who had helped throughout the process. Ed Shield, of PSE, had overseen much of the transition from hydroelectric power to shutting down the century old system in 2004. He recalled the history of the plant, and officially turned over the "keys" of the entire White River Lake Tapps project to Cascade. "I can now do this with great optimism for the future," Shield said. "This is quite a system and it's good to know it will be in good hands."

Accepting the handoff for Cascade were Board Chair Lloyd Warren and CEO Chuck Clarke who promised that they'd take good care of the system and the community. Following the transfer of ownership, Auburn

Cascade's Lloyd Warren officially accepts the keys to the Lake Tapps project from Ed Shield of PSE

Mayor Pete Lewis, Bonney Lake Mayor Neil Johnson, Buckley Mayor Pat Johnson and Sumner Mayor Dave Enslow and Cascade representatives signed the newly minted Lake Tapps Area Water Resources Agreement. This deal assured the four communities around the reservoir that they would have water for their residents for decades.

Wrapping up the meeting were Lake Tapps Community Council representatives Chuck Romeo and Leon Stucki. Long time leaders and fierce proponents of the lake and avid protectors of its recreational lake levels, the two acknowledged they had fought the good fight and thanked Cascade for meeting them and working together to save their beloved lake.

Prior to the adjournment of the final meeting of the Lake Tapps Task Force, Hilyer said, "Now, having achieved our stated objectives of this effort—to save Lake Tapps—I conclude the work of this group and declare our work complete." A cake was brought forth that simply yet powerfully proclaimed the phrase "Celebrating New Beginnings."

Lloyd Warren, Cascade's chair, spoke for Cascade. "In 1980, a number of us got together to begin a decade-long dialogue about water—about protecting our future and creating our destiny. That discussion became Cascade. Now, 30 years later, we all stand here together, as neighbors, as a community, as partners. Our strength is a shared vision of water

Top: Cascade's Grant Degginger with Lake Tapps Community Council President Chuck Romeo; Above: Lake Tapps' Leon Stucki

Heralding the regional collaboration and partnerships were Cong. Dave Reichert, left, and now Gov. Jay Inslee

for today and tomorrow. It's been quite a journey as we all struggled to meet our unique individual water supply needs while capitalizing on our collective strength; the Tribes, the homeowners and the cities. We make good partners. Our work will serve the region well. This will be our home. We really feel a part of the neighborhood. The Task Force always has a cake celebration to commemorate its milestones. I would say this ranks as a milestone, wouldn't you?"

Celebrating with the Lake Tapps community were Congressmen Dave Reichert, Jay Inslee (elected Washington Governor in 2012) and Adam Smith, and King County Executive Dow Constantine. Cong. Reichert congratulated the group on demonstrating what regional partnerships are all about and what they can accomplish. Cong. Smith added that threats sometimes bring people together to accomplish what they might not have been able to do otherwise. Inslee recognized Cascade for bringing cities together to get water for the future and forging regional planning along the way.

Executive Constantine added that from Redmond to Lake Tapps, steps the people in that tent took that day will lead to infrastructure for tomorrow. "The region is better off for your partnerships and planning." Warren concluded by giving Michelle Shuler, a member at large of the Lake Tapps Task Force, the honor of cutting the cake.

TAPPING INTO AN ASSET

WATER enough for the next 50 years. Those are unimaginable words in parts of the country, and even in the rainy Northwest they are cause for celebration.

Now the cities of Auburn, Bonney Lake, Buckley and Sumner can anticipate adequate water supplies out to 2060. Another landmark agreement has been reached on the future of Lake Tapps by the Cascade Water Alliance.

Lake Tapps, south of Auburn in Pierce County, was created nearly 100 years ago to power a hydroelectric dam. Cascade purchased the lake from Puget Sound Energy when it stopped generating electricity in 2004. The reservoir is a valuable long-term source of drinking water.

Management of the lake, fed by the White River, has been a constant topic of negotiations since Cascade, a consortium of five cities and three municipal water districts, and PSE sought to close a deal.

In the agreement signed on Friday, Cascade agreed to leave water in the White River that will be available to the four cities to use if they receive a water right from the state Department of Ecology. The cities would also be eligible for some of the existing water supply provided by Tacoma Public Utilities.

Cascade, which serves 370,000 residents and 22,000 businesses east and south of Lake Washington, has been working to maximize the benefit from "a wonderful regional asset," in the words of Auburn Mayor Pete Lewis.

Cascade had previously worked out agreements in 2008 with the Puyallup and Muckleshoot tribes to protect salmon runs. In decades past, diversions from the White River had reduced its flow to a trickle. Last spring Cascade and the Lake Tapps Community Council ended years of tough negotiations about the dual use of the lake as a water supply and recreational amenity.

Dozens of city, state and federal dignitaries gathered to celebrate the moment on Friday because good news for Auburn, Bonney Lake, Buckley and Sumner extends to the region.

KEN LAMBERT / THE SEATTLE TIMES
Water diverted from the White River heads toward Lake Tapps

From *The Seattle Times*

THE WORD AND RECOGNITION SPREAD

That week the Seattle Times editorialized the partnerships in a piece called "Tapping into an Asset."

> "Water enough for the next 50 years. Those are unimaginable words in many parts of the country and even in the rainy Northwest are cause for celebration. Another landmark agreement has been reached on the future of Lake Tapps by Cascade Water Alliance…to maximize the benefit from 'a wonderful regional asset'," in the words of Auburn Mayor Pete Lewis.

Pete Lewis and Lloyd Warren co-authored a piece in the Auburn Reporter on Feb. 5 agreeing that "we can tell you this was not an easy process. It was a protracted series of tough negotiations. But we can also tell you that it is regional leadership at its best. We are proud of the results of our efforts to make sure Lake Tapps remains the wonderful regional jewel it is while we provide water for decades to come for all of our citizens. Cascade is a welcome part of this community."

Cascade continues to be a good partner with the Lake Tapps community. Following this event it held a meeting for residents to come discuss Cascade's ongoing intent to continue to work closely with the residents. It also sponsored local events. But Cascade wanted to make a broader statement and thank the entire community, including individuals who lived around the lake, residents to whom Lake Tapps was a big part of their own lives. So on Oct. 5, 2011, Cascade held yet another celebration to commemorate the centennial of the powerhouse on East Valley Highway. Many residents said they had never seen the inside of the imposing building, and so Cascade threw open the doors for tours of the facility.

Cascade promised hotdogs for anyone interested, so the barbecues were fired up. A local band and a clown entertained the crowd, and of course there had to be more cake. While about 150 were expected, more than 500 people showed up, going on tours of the powerhouse and

Opposite: Cascade's imposing powerhouse— inside and out

eating every bit of the food. Residents, who claimed they had driven by the powerhouse for all of their lives, excitedly checked out every nook and cranny and operations of the century old building.

The Tacoma News Tribune noted attendees gathered to "reminisce, to eat, to listen to music of an old time acoustic speakeasy swing band and finally to tour the powerhouse plant that has stood since 1911… It's a piece of history."

In 2012, community member Robyn Sullivan "rescued" one of the original Lake Tapps Development Company signs, and relocated it to the powerhouse property. And to further cement the powerhouse location as a site for the area's history, a new historical marker was unveiled and dedicated on May 19, 2012, marking the powerhouse as a "significant community resource." A new marker was placed by the Greater Bonney Lake Historical Society which had already dedicated ten other sites in the area in 2009. The marker says that "what was begun over a century ago at Lake Tapps has a new beginning with its purchase in 2009 by Cascade Water Alliance as a future municipal water supply."

Marking history at the powerhouse

Dedicating the Lake Tapps White River Project as one of historical significance to the region

The Lake Tapps White River Project

In response to the ever increasing demand for electrical power in the Seattle-Tacoma region during the early 20th century, a plan was proposed by Pacific Coast Power Company to utilize the natural terrain of the plateau to generate hydroelectric power. In 1910 the "White River Power Project" was launched. It created a large reservoir by flooding four of the existing lakes, Kirtley, Crawford, Church, and Tapps, to create a much larger Lake Tapps. This flooding was accomplished by building approximately 2.5 miles of earthen dikes which raised the water level by 35 feet, thereby joining the lakes together.

By diverting water from the White River through a diversion dam near Buckley, it was channeled through a series of basins and wooden flumes to the reservoir. The water then traveled north through the lake to a penstock tunnel, where it exited at the White River Power station at Dieringer. After running through the turbines which created the magic of electricity, the water then rejoined the river west of Dieringer and continued to the Puyallup River and Puget Sound. The resulting 14 mile long lake required some 20 million board feet of lumber to complete the necessary miles of flumes, canal linings, and rail trestles. It was an amazing feat that was accomplished in just twenty months by an average of one thousand men in seventeen camps located along the plateau.

The power station has since been closed, but picturesque 2,566 acre Lake Tapps remains. What was begun over a century ago at Lake Tapps has a new beginning with its purchase in 2009 by Cascade Water Alliance as a future municipal water supply. Agreements with residents, the local tribes and neighboring cities mean a future with sustainable water for people, water for fish, and water for recreation.

This Historic Marker was funded by Cascade Water Alliance in celebration of the
Centennial of the Lake Tapps White River Project
1911 – 2011

11.
COALITION BUILDING AND LEGISLATIVE FIXES

Throughout this journey, Cascade developed good working relationships with critical stakeholders at Lake Tapps, but there were some festering wounds around the water community dating back decades. These tenuous bonds still needed to be addressed because Cascade had learned well the value of important partnerships and relationship building.

In 2009, Cascade was facing two major obstacles—one was regulatory, the other organizational. The first involved Cascade's need to draw up a plan to get water to its members. Cascade had to create a Transmission and Supply Plan (TSP) by 2012 as required by the State Department of Health. Getting all the approvals and the support, or at best neutrality, from agencies that could impact negatively on the plan made the effort more daunting. The second hurdle was getting the required franchise agreement with King County. Staff and attorneys were having little luck and even less progress towards that effort. The question was how best to tackle these challenges and move forward.

Building on all Cascade had learned from its earlier outreach efforts—that working with stakeholders and partners makes regional actions easier—Cascade refreshed the approach to its planning efforts. As the Transmission Plan was being developed, Cascade decided to involve those who would most likely be presenting comments ahead of introducing a plan.

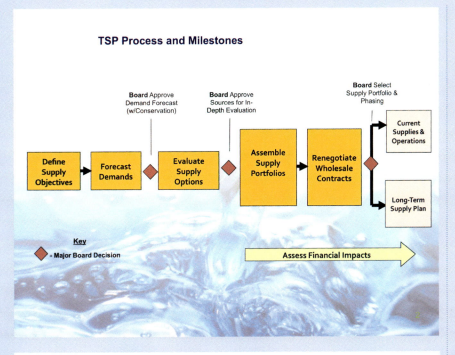

Examples of presentations at the Connections Working Group

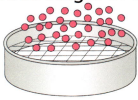
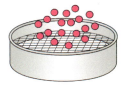

Cascade reached out to more than 30 stakeholders from cities, counties, state agencies, business, environmental groups and land use communities, neighborhood groups and most importantly other utilities in the region, and invited them to a series of meetings over the next 18 months to hear about Cascade's planning efforts. Many were the water purveyors who were not fans of Cascade from the original planning process a decade earlier. Some of those purveyors were still outright hostile. Several that were invited didn't know anything about Cascade and its plans, including those who might impact the franchise agreement or actual transmission. Then there were those just interested in what Cascade might have to say and a few who simply wondered why they were asked to attend. Cascade called this loosely gathered crowd the "Connections Working Group."

Michael Gagliardo makes a presentation to the group

> Cascade knew it was critical to make the process informative and substantive, yet transparent and credible. Also important was to give the group something tangible to react to, and the real ability and even responsibility for input in the decision making. In other words, it would empower the Connections Working Group with a voice.

The effort was staffed by Michael Gagliardo and Andrew Graham of HDR, but it was facilitated independently by consultants from Katz and Associates, a well-respected water industry outreach firm from San Diego. Neither Gagliardo nor Graham were initially comfortable with this approach. Traditionally, the only outreach done on such plans had been the advertising notices required by state statute. As final decisions hadn't been made, the Cascade board hesitated to share the options under consideration. After long and honest conversations, it was clear that this tactic could only enhance key stakeholders' involvement and engagement of those who could have an impact on the TSP's eventual approval and adoption. It was decided to go ahead. No other utility had opened its planning process to outside entities, other than what was required in the way of public notices. Although not thrilled with the decision, Gagliardo and Graham nonetheless prepared thorough, complete and detailed materials for the first meeting.

Andrew Graham of HDR

Cascade knew it was critical to make the process informative and substantive, yet transparent and credible. Also important was to give the group something tangible to react to, and the real ability and even responsibility for input in the decision making. In other words, it would empower the Connections Working Group with a voice.

Cascade focused on supply and demand and shared all the information Cascade was using in making its analyses—charts, graphs and data. It previewed potential water sources and transmission alternatives.

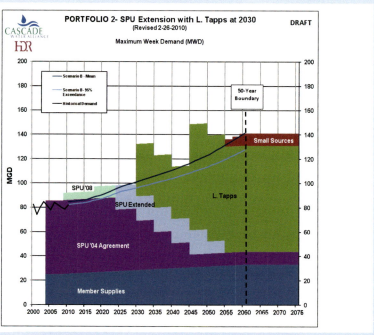

Examples of the data Cascade shared

It shared the criteria it proposed to determine which decisions would make the most environmental, water supply, political and economic sense.

Participants attended morning-long meetings in which Cascade previewed its entire planning process and the options being considered. Attendees were given the materials to review before each meeting and then asked Cascade tough, challenging questions. Follow up information and answers to questions was sent immediately after each meeting. At the beginning of the next meeting, attendees were asked if there was understanding and agreement that Cascade had answered their previous questions or if there was additional work that needed to be done. Only after attendees said they were satisfied with the information did the group move on.

Cascade, committed to the transparency efforts that had worked so well around Lake Tapps, put it all on the table, striving to make every consideration, action and decision clear to attendees. By the end of the first Connections Working Group meeting, Gagliardo and Graham saw the wisdom of the plan and they respected the critical input participants offered that helped make each subsequent meeting more effective.

Each meeting reflected exactly what the Cascade board was examining, and the group's insightful comments and questions were often reported back and eventually incorporated into the planning documents. Major input was passed along to the board for consideration in its final planning decisions.

However, during the months-long process, Cascade also began receiving new information that was changing its thinking. Water demand was decreasing, not just for Cascade but for all water suppliers in the region. True to the commitment of transparency, Cascade shared this information with the Connections Working Group.

It was not lost on this group, Cascade, its board or engineer consultants that if Cascade was experiencing this, other regional utilities, like Seattle and Tacoma might be as well, and that they might be willing to sell their excess water to Cascade. Cascade had the ability to pay for water. Other utilities needed funds for their infrastructure needs. Would

> "The result of the Connections Working Group was that stakeholders understood, supported and even affirmed the change in direction. The group supported Cascade's efforts to work with Seattle and Tacoma utilities to see if they could come to agreements on how to best maximize all existing water in the region before beginning any future development of Lake Tapps," said Chuck Clarke.

the development of municipal water supply from Lake Tapps and major transmission supply systems even be necessary?

"The result of the Connections Working Group was that stakeholders understood, supported and even affirmed the change in direction. The group supported Cascade's efforts to work with Seattle and Tacoma utilities to see if they could come to agreements on how to best maximize all existing water in the region before beginning any future development of Lake Tapps," said Chuck Clarke.

It meant that with as much available water in the region, developing Lake Tapps for water supply was not necessary now or in the foreseeable

Participants at the Connections Working Group

future—or perhaps not at all. Cascade revised its plans to reflect this as the group's work proceeded. All efforts to obtain a franchise from King County were halted. Cascade would not be building a transmission system anytime soon so did not need a franchise. The stakeholder input had helped identify a better way for everyone. The Connections Working Group had been a part of the decision making and supported the new plan. It issued a report to the Cascade board in December 2010.

Walt Canter, a long time Cedar River Water and Sewer District commissioner in the region, had not been a strong advocate for Cascade prior to this effort. He acknowledged he was downright skeptical. But as the Connections Working Group tasks were completed and the report was prepared, he spoke for the group as it transmitted its report. He felt Cascade's transparency went a long way towards understanding, collaboration and future cooperation in the region. The result, he said, was credibility for Cascade.

In late 2010, Cascade shelved its plans for quickly developing Lake Tapps and initiated efforts with Seattle and Tacoma to revise contracts for the purchase of water. This officially put future development of Lake Tapps on hold for decades. It also led Cascade to review and modify its own internal cost allocations and demand shares to make sure its growing members paid their fair share through connections and their use of water. Equitable distribution of costs, with each member paying its fair share, meant Cascade's growth paid for growth in a just manner.

Despite not moving forward with actual development, the outcome of the transparent planning process had a major impact. Cascade had created a sense of trust throughout the region, putting to bed many old hostilities. Reaching out had built a bond among key stakeholders, but especially among water providers. As a result, Cascade established a new water supply agreement with Tacoma in December 2012 and a new declining water supply agreement with Seattle in July 2013.

Not developing Lake Tapps in the near term, and working with the others to purchase their existing water, benefited everyone environmentally and financially. More importantly, it created a win-win in the region and solidified the relationship between Cascade and the other major water providers—Seattle, Tacoma and Everett. And, by getting even the crankiest antagonists to the table and turning them into Cascade supporters, Cascade could now move forward in a positive and proactive manner with allies as it considered its next steps as a regional water provider.

Cascade had established itself as a credible entity. It had engendered trust and transparency with previous skeptics. And it had shown a leadership role in the region by working with others to maximize available water use rather than pursuing its own agenda. With this and owning a major water supply source, Cascade became an equal player among the major water providers of the region. But because it did not operate a utility, it had the opportunity to do other work to benefit the water community in a larger arena. It had finally become widely acknowledged as a major regional water partner.

A FOCUS ON STRUCTURE

Lessons learned from this process, the trust that had been earned and the leadership it was demonstrating paved the way for the next steps in Cascade's evolution. Steps that were equally important for the region and the state. Born out of the need for legislative changes to organizational shortcomings, and with leadership at the water supply level, Cascade next tackled state fixes that would have an impact for many and great results for all.

By having a small staff and an active board, Cascade was able to be nimble and respond quickly to differing conditions. But it still faced a major, lingering issue that had plagued it since its inception… its form of government. In 2004, State Senator Jim Honeyford created legislation based on the Interlocal Act as a method of issuing bonds as a funding mechanism for certain entities. Hugh Spitzer, the respected municipal attorney, improved the bill and created a watershed management for Honeyford's purposes. Though it didn't pan out for that effort, Spitzer's work expanded the bill to allow for future projects that could use this provision to include municipal water supply. With no other options, this

Cascade board members. Top: Jon Ault, left and Mary Alyce Burleigh center; Above: Ault and Lloyd Warren

is the mechanism Cascade used when it became a management partnership in 2004.

Yet what did that really mean? Questions abounded about Cascade's status, such as, is Cascade a non-profit or a governmental entity? Can it contract with additional governments under the Interlocal Cooperation Act? Are its employees "public employees" eligible for participation in various pension and benefits programs? Which public works, procurement and surplus property laws apply? What federal and state tax exemptions are available? Would risk management and protections for local governments apply to interlocal agencies? Did Cascade function as efficiently as possible? It was clear that its structure and its needs were not a perfect fit.

As early as 2008, Cascade began running into these issues and more as new financial and administrative policies and procedures began being implemented. Up until now, Cascade had been patching together a legal framework for the organization by addressing each issue as it arose—an effort that proved costly and time consuming.

If other local utility agencies wanted to organize into regional efforts, they would face the same challenges because of the lack of certainty regarding their ability to jointly exercise authority and/or the ambiguous status of intergovernmental entities created under the state's interlocal cooperation act. Cascade board members realized that clarifications were needed, but were unsure how to start.

During the 2010 Legislature, Cascade began to raise questions about clarifying legal authority of such entities. Thurston County's LOTT Clean Water Alliance (Lacey, Olympia, Tumwater and Thurston County) joined in the discussion as they, too, wanted to get clarifications on the key questions facing these two entities.

Cascade introduced a bill calling for a study measure to identify

> Cascade had created a list of 23 issues members felt should be examined, ranging from franchises, grants, eminent domain, contracts, risk management, insurance, financing and bonding, taxes and governing. Were others interested? Would others concur? Would there be other issues?

and address these issues. Although the legislation wasn't adopted, it caught the attention of the State Department of Ecology Director Ted Sturdevant. He understood that local governments that provide water, wastewater, stormwater and/or flood controls services face serious roadblocks to their ability to provide essential public services. So, he spoke with Ken Slattery, now retired Program Manager of the Water Resources Program at Ecology and Denise Clifford, Department of Health's Director of the Office of Drinking Water. They all agreed the questions had merit and together the agencies launched an exploratory effort. The State Departments of Ecology and Health convened a group of water related utilities to see if there was sufficient interest to address these issues. They focused on existing or potentially new regional organizations that would deliver essential water related public services.

A DIFFERENT KIND OF OUTREACH MEETING

The two departments sent out a letter to all potentially interested agencies in the state. Cascade contacted utilities and other governmental entities, urging them to join the meeting, which was set for July 9, 2010 at 2 p.m.—a sunny summer Friday afternoon—in Olympia. Cascade staff and lobbyists gathered in the sun-filled conference room and set up a conference call line in case anyone called in. Cascade had created a list of 23 issues members felt should be examined, ranging from franchises, grants, eminent domain, contracts, risk management, insurance, financing and bonding, taxes and governing. Were others interested? Would others concur? Would there be other issues? Might there be any interest by anyone other than Cascade and LOTT?

Legal expert Hugh Spitzer

Shortly before the meeting started, the room began to fill. The conference phone line buzzed continually. From around the state, about two dozen agencies participated. It seemed those same concerns Cascade had worried about hit a common cord with others.

"The issues were broad and affected many agencies," said Cindy Zehnder, former chief of staff to Gov. Christine Gregoire, currently with Gordon Thomas Honeywell, Cascade's lobbying firm in Olympia.

Some small entities in Lewis County, Vader and Toledo, were concerned that they couldn't separately provide all services and were wondering if a collective entity could better serve their residents. Others from Spokane and Clark Counties were in the process of organizing. Many had specific problems with procurement, surplus or other issues.

"It became clear there were consistent and compelling issues," said Adam Gravley of VanNess Feldman, who, with Hugh Spitzer, listened to the agencies' discussion as they pondered whether there was a basis for potential legislation.

The answer was clearly yes. At the conclusion of the first meeting, it was decided by the group to proceed to identify issues and potential solutions. The group also limited the scope of any future resolutions to existing water related entities. Spitzer, one of the main drafters of this legislation, understood the potential use of such legislation, so he wrote it in a manner that other entities could adapt legislation to address similar concerns specific to whatever their respective issue would be.

Cascade worked with the Washington Association of Water and Sewer Districts (WASWD) and the Washington Water Utilities Council (WWUC). Their memberships' buy-in, contributions and support for the effort was critical in moving forward. Without it there would have been little credibility for the potential legislation. Blair Burroughs of WASWD, Randy Black of WWUC and John Kounts of the Washington Association of Public Utility Districts (WAPUD) led their organizations to understand and support the process.

"What the measure would do," said Zehnder, who facilitated the process, "was make it easier for entities to provide essential services to the public more efficiently and more cost effectively. What we did was make everyone comfortable with what we were proposing."

Cascade lobbyist Cindy Zehnder

IT'S A GO

A second meeting was set for Aug. 19 in Olympia. The group had grown and participants were eager to proceed. Subsequently, this group of more than 30 agencies met over a period of six months. This statewide collaborative process produced clarifying legislation that would be voluntary and did not grant any new powers. Many entities sent their lobbyists, legal counsel and staff to a work group that drafted the final proposed measure. Others participated to fully understand the potential impact of such legislation, and still others wanted to make sure it did not impact them.

"What the measure would do," said Zehnder, who facilitated the process, "was make it easier for entities to provide essential services to the public more efficiently and more cost effectively. What we did was make everyone comfortable with what we were proposing."

The outcome of the work was twofold. First, and perhaps most critical in the process, was that every entity felt heard. Nothing included in the legislation was adopted without the group's buy-in. Each question was raised, discussed and reviewed with the entire group, and the bill drafters explained how and why they had prepared key aspects of the bill to address each point. Second was that the work product was ultimately endorsed and supported by the entire membership of the group—they all had a collective vision.

After much review, the members of the newly minted "joint municipal utility services" coalition arrived at a proposed new statute that focused narrowly on addressing issues and challenges as they apply to municipal utilities. It was intended to facilitate joint municipal utility services but not intended to expand the types of services provided by local governments or their utilities. Nothing in the act altered the underlying authority of the units of local governments that entered into agreements under the act or in any way diminished that authority.

"For the effort to be successful, we need to be unified on the bill and the approach to getting it through the session," Zehnder said.

It's a go, the group said. By the time November and December rolled around, the gathered entities had endorsements from their governing bodies to support House Bill 1332, providing for the joint provision and management of municipal water, wastewater, storm and flood water and related utility services. The bill called for the authority to create a Joint Municipal Utilities Services Authority (JMUSA).

TAKING IT TO OLYMPIA

State Rep. Deb Eddy, a Democrat from Kirkland, stepped forward to serve as the sponsor of the measure. Having served as president of the region's Suburban Cities Association, and as a tireless advocate of partnerships to make government more efficient, she was an ideal sponsor. "We have local governments that are willing and wanting to serve their residents more efficiently and at a lower cost. We should make it easier, not harder, for these groups to work together, especially when the end result could mean a lower utility bill for ratepayers," said Eddy.

> "We have local governments that are willing and wanting to serve their residents more efficiently and at a lower cost. We should make it easier, not harder, for these groups to work together, especially when the end result could mean a lower utility bill for ratepayers," said Eddy.

A legislative strategy session was held Dec. 10, 2010 in Olympia for agencies, their lobbyists and the drafters of the legislation to work together to move the bill forward. A hearing was set before the House Local Government Committee in Olympia on Jan. 26, 2011. The number of groups or individuals signing in to testify or show support filled three pages, and all indicated they were in favor of the bill.

A carefully identified cross-section of the group was selected to testify—utilities, water districts and the lead author of the measure, Hugh Spitzer. When committee members saw the list of those testifying, and the respected Spitzer before them, they were impressed at the collective gathering in support of the bill. They were also confident of its being thorough and well written, as it was drafted by Spitzer. After some minor and acceptable tweaks, the substitute bill passed the committee two days later and soon the full House, 92 to 0.

State Rep. Deb Eddy

The measure was sent to the Senate Committee on Governmental Operations and Tribal Relations and Elections. It was heard March 8, 2011 with similar fanfare as in the House. After minor alterations, the measure was passed out of committee March 15 and passed in the Senate 40 to 8.

The House concurred with the Senate amendments and passed the bill 95 to 1 on April 15. Once signed by the Speaker of the House, the bill was sent to Gov. Christine Gregoire and she signed it into law May 5,

2011. Cascade had gotten the legislative changes it needed to be a more effective and efficient organization. The bill:

- Creates a Joint Municipal Utility Services Authority by two or more members to perform or provide any or all of the utility services that all of its members perform or provide. Members can be a county, city, town, special purpose district or local government in Washington agreeing to form an authority. Utility services are retail or wholesale water supply and conservation services, wastewater sewage, or disposal services and the management of storm, surface, draining and flood waters;
- Authorizes formed municipal corporations to perform services its members perform or provide, with immunities and exceptions that apply to local government entities; and
- Allows Joint Municipal Utility Services Authorities to sue, acquire property, incur liabilities, issue bonds, receive public and private monies and assistance, employ individuals, fix salaries, determine fees, rates and charges for services, and use eminent domain. They can also transfer assets and water rights, they can form a new entity, and they can convert an existing entity or entities into joint authorities.

JMUSA become a reality as the bill is signed into law

Once the bill was signed into law, Cascade began the process of converting from a watershed management partnership to a Joint Municipal Utilities Authority. It adopted the measures necessary at the board level to make the changes and its members got the approval from their governing bodies. On July 12, 2012, Cascade filed with the Washington State Secretary of State to officially become the state's first municipal corporation under JMUSA.

AN IDENTITY FOR ADVOCACY

With its new status, Cascade would become an even more efficient, effective organization. However, it got much more out of this process than its initial goal of being a better entity. Its credibility and trustworthiness grew exponentially. Cascade became known for fairness, advocacy and innovative approaches to problem solving. It was also now being viewed as a leader that could build regional coalitions focusing on major issues. Cascade took this role as convener seriously, and it was only a few months later that it was pressed into service again as a statewide convener.

In the summer of 2012, during one of Cascade's Public Affairs Committee meetings, some of Cascade's city utilities and water and sewer district members mentioned they were dealing with a perplexing issue. Two recent State Supreme Court decisions (Lane vs. City of Seattle and City of Bonney Lake vs. City of Tacoma) had been issued. Each ruling dealt with who pays for fire hydrants, what costs may be recovered and the mechanism or process that may be used for cost recovery. The problem was the rulings were contradictory.

Cascade knew that if its districts and its cities were concerned, others might be as well. It soon became clear that there was much confusion and consternation about the impacts of these cases on operations, financing and liability statewide.

Cascade was right that other entities shared these concerns. These unresolved issues prompted Cascade and others across the state to initiate a process similar to the JMUSA effort. Because trust had been established

> After a successful effort with JMUSA, many of the same parties came back to the table, greeting each other as successful warriors with a win under their belts ready to tackle a new and equally perplexing issue. Joining the effort, however, were newcomers who were understandably skeptical.

that Cascade and the Zehnder-run processes were fair and productive, Cascade was urged to lead this work. Participants, entities, organizations and municipalities that had been slow to join the effort a year before, jumped immediately forward and agreed to come together to determine next steps.

The Washington Water Utilities Council, in conjunction with Cascade, held a meeting to implement a statewide fire protection outreach effort to address possible solutions to these two decisions heading into the 2013 Legislative Session. Interested parties were invited to gather for the first meeting of the Fire Protection and Liability and Security Working Group (Fire PALS.) All interested parties were encouraged to attend and bring stakeholders to the table to ensure an all-inclusive process. The first meeting was held Aug. 16, 2012 at Gordon Thomas Honeywell's Tacoma offices. The goal was to determine who pays for fire hydrants, what costs may be recovered, liability protection and the mechanism that may be used for cost recovery.

After a successful effort with JMUSA, many of the same parties came back to the table, greeting each other as successful warriors with a win under their belts ready to tackle a new and equally perplexing issue. Joining the effort, however, were newcomers who were understandably skeptical. Having only come to observe, these Fire Marshalls, Fire Chiefs' associations and other fire protection interests, some in full uniform dress, gathered on one side of the table. There they sat quietly, watching the chatty gathering of water providers and municipalities.

Cindy Zehnder reprised her role as the impartial facilitator and began with introductions. The warm welcome worked its way across the massive conference table that filled the entire room. Each entity explained the challenges it was facing and what it was seeking from this process. The answers were far ranging, but all felt the current status was unworkable and financially risky. Some of those uniformed fire personnel admitted that they had come to protect their members and their interests, expecting a fight. But, after hearing the issues around the room, they said they shared the same concerns. Everyone quickly got to work. The group established an agenda, key issues, concerns and potential solutions.

Because this was a second collective effort in just two years, the group was very comfortable charging the same talented team of attorneys who had worked so diligently on JMUSA to again work together and come back to the group with options for members to review. The attorneys worked feverishly. The whole group met twice in September—the first time on Sept. 13 to review possible solutions and the second on Sep. 27 to discuss potential legislative solutions. By Oct. 11, Hugh Spitzer and his capable cadre of attorneys, including Adam Gravley, Jon Milne, Tom Brubaker (Kent), Kristin Lamson (Seattle) and others drafted options for legislative language.

Unfortunately, the questions of who pays and who is responsible for fire protection threatened to break up the group. Zehnder again reiterated that the group could only go forward if this critical issue could be addressed. Without it, any proposed legislation would have no teeth and would likely die right there in the conference room. So, participants went back to their governing bodies and returned with issues that had surfaced. Included in the list were findings and purpose, cost recovery and authority confirmation, protection of siting arrangements and a liability protection provision. The attorneys worked quickly to incorporate and address those issues and by Nov. 13, a draft had been hammered out that the diverse group of interests could agree on.

Much thought had been given as to how to approach the Legislature, which might be hesitant to overturn or counter the State Supreme Court. The unanimous approach suggested by the attorney work group was to offer these provisions as clarifications that would help public health and safety organizations comply with the previous rulings and yet still be protected from liability and budgetary constraints.

"It was clear that Cascade's knowledge of the issues, excellent key stakeholder relationships built over many years of exemplary service, staff leadership and great communication skills had much to do with these successes. I see Cascade continuing this role as convener on other issues in the future."

The next step was to establish a legislative strategy and meet with participants' lobbyists. Members who had worked with Cascade on the JMUSA process felt like old hands at this part of the process.

From the effort that began with more than 50 individuals representing a diverse group of organizations had come House Bill 1512 sponsored by State. Rep. Dean Takko. It was to be heard before the House Local Government Committee on Feb. 8, 2013. Fire PALS had selected a representative from utilities, city representatives (one large, one small, one Western Washington and one Eastern Washington) to testify and asked Spitzer to again speak to the technical components of the legislation. The undisputed choice to represent the fire interests was an officer in uniform—Beau Bakken, fire chief at North Mason Regional Fire Authority. The list of those signing in support of the legislation was long, inclusive and impressive—even more so with this piece of legislation because of the variety of interests pursuing a remedy.

Although Spitzer carried instant credibility in the room of legislators, and the number of supporters and lack of opponents was impressive to lawmakers, the most compelling figure was Bakken. He testified that should fire protection be needed in any corner of the state, it was imperative that water districts and municipalities be able to provide the water fire fighters would need. This measure addressed all concerns, allowing those who had already adopted or reached workable solutions to keep them, but also offered solutions to others who had struggled.

The bill was quickly passed out of committee on Feb. 12 and sent to the full House where it passed 97 to 0 on March 4, 2013.

The process was repeated in the Senate at the Senate Committee on Governmental Operations on March 25, and it passed to the full Senate on April 1. The bill passed April 15, 45 to 3 and sent to the Governor for signature. On May 3, 2013, with more than two dozen supporters behind him, Gov. Jay Inslee signed the measure into law, assuring all Fire PALS and their respective jurisdictions that fire protection, its safety, liability and financial future was clarified, codified and guaranteed.

Cascade had done it again. For the second time it got the ball rolling on critical, complex and much-needed statewide legislation. It had shown itself as a coalition builder and leader in the state. Cascade was recognized as a convener able to bring about change with critical stakeholders and elected officials on ground breaking efforts. Cindy Zehnder added, "It was clear that Cascade's knowledge of the issues, excellent key stakeholder relationships built over many years of exemplary service, staff leadership and great communication skills had much to do with these successes. I see Cascade continuing this role as convener on other issues in the future."

Gov. Jay Inslee signing Fire PALS legislation into law on May 3, 2013

12.
RESCUING THE RESERVOIR; WATER FOR THE FUTURE

By late 2009, Cascade needed someone special to manage its Lake Tapps operations. So, interviewing began for the newly created and critically important Lake Tapps Operations Manager position.

The interviewers included, among others, newly hired Cascade engineer Jon Shimada, from Seattle Public Utilities, an expert in asset management, and Darryl Grigsby, from the City of Kirkland. A list of ten questions was established for the interview process.

One candidate, Joe Mickelson, began his career as a journey level baker at 19, and had joined Seattle Water District when he was just 22. He worked his way up to crew chief, watershed operations director on the Tolt and Cedar Rivers and in North Bend. He had even worked for Chuck Clarke during Clarke's tenure at Seattle Public Utilities. Mickelson had gotten where he was because he knew what he was doing on the job. He had been called on to work day and night, speak to the media and, where needed, jump in a ditch and fix things himself. He was a "get 'er done" kind of guy.

Mickelson, a very large six-foot three current world champion super heavy-weight bench press and dead lift champion, made an impression the moment he came in for his interview. Introductions were made, and he was asked the first question: Tell us how your experiences in Seattle might translate to this new job?

The interview panel never had to ask another question. The warm, open and incredibly personable Mickelson shared his career highlights

Cascade's Lake Tapps Operations Manager Joe Mickelson

and the activities of which he was proudest. He noted that he'd only taken two sick days in his 30-year career at Seattle—one day each for the birth of his two children. His father had also been a career Seattle Public Utilities employee.

His work ethic and abilities were already well known to Clarke and Shimada, and his sincerity was contagious and engaging. Cascade's criteria for this position was how this person would work with the Lake Tapps Community. After spending about three minutes with him there was absolutely no doubt in the interviewers' minds that Joe was a great fit for both Cascade and the Lake Tapps folks.

The universal consensus was that Joe was a winner—the right guy for the job. Soon after Joe was hired, he had quite the unique opportunity to show everyone that no matter what the challenge, he was true to his own personal motto of "get 'er done."

But, even with his charm and experience, the task in front of him was daunting. Lake Tapps and the entire White River project was more than 100 years old. Cascade had accepted the project from Puget Sound Energy "as is." It included 12 miles of flumes, conveyances, pipes, gates, 15 dikes and a 44,000 acre feet reservoir which 1,700 lakefront residents called home.

> Mickelson admitted that he occasionally wondered exactly what he had gotten himself into. How could Cascade accomplish everything that needed to be done? The project tested every skill set he had—and more.

"When I first went down to Lake Tapps with Jon (Shimada)—I didn't even know where it was. When I saw the entire White River system, it was like walking back into 1960. Nothing had been upgraded, there was no computerized management system, no paperwork, manuals, and documentation on equipment or inventory."

PSE crews managed every aspect of this infrastructure, from building to electronics and more. But after the company decided to sell the system, maintenance was reduced. There were no manuals or procedures, and while there was a lot of history, nothing was written down. Cascade had done a high level assessment prior to the purchase but it didn't address things like lead paint, electrical, maintenance, vegetation management or proper equipment status. With no information, Cascade struggled to make good decisions and ended up just making fixes and doing work as necessary. It was apparent that the time had come to develop a complete asset management system and do an entire overhaul of the system.

MAKING A PLAN

"I had to hit the ground running and learn the system as I worked the system," Joe said. Five PSE staff had been left to assist in the transition. After PSE's Snoqualmie site was shut down some additional staff came to help. "There was a list of 60 electrical issues alone, and so much in disrepair that needed upgrading," he continued. "Plus, I do all kinds of routine things like change all the locks—$8,000 worth! But I know from working with Chuck and listening to the Cascade board that Cascade wanted to set a very high standard for its work."

Mickelson quickly discovered that several quick fixes were needed—lots of spit, tape and glue. But it was also clear to him that a major overhaul would be needed for the system to operate well over the long

> "We developed a plan of how we had to do all the work and sequence the projects—electrical, the flume, the headgates, dikes, powerhouse and so much more. We wanted to impact homeowners only once so we obtained funding and went to the community to tell them the news," Mickelson said.

haul. He explained that the structure "needed a new flume—the old one was rotting. We needed new fish screens. We needed a complete system assessment, because there might be things we didn't see."

Mickelson admitted that he occasionally wondered exactly what he had gotten himself into. How could Cascade accomplish everything that needed to be done? The project tested every skill set he had—and more.

Cascade set up a meeting for Mickelson to meet the Lake Tapps Community Council—Chuck Romeo, Leon Stucki, Ralph Mason and Ken Castile. "I hit it off right away with Chuck, but I had to work a little harder to prove myself to Leon," Mickelson shared. "So I listened to them and I followed through and got them results. We developed wonderful relationships. A great addition to this group was John Clark, who manages Tapps Island. I remember Ralph later told me that he was glad Cascade bought Lake Tapps because it required way more than the homeowners could have done."

Cascade took over all operations, kept PSE's Gene Galloway, and hired Veolia Construction, Inc. to manage them. A project list of major improvements grew steadily and by 2013, it was clear the time had come to do the major work.

"We developed a plan of how we had to do all the work and sequence the projects—electrical, the flume, the headgates, dikes, powerhouse and so much more. We wanted to impact homeowners only once so we obtained funding and went to the community to tell them the news," Mickelson said.

One other task Mickelson was very good at, but was hesitant to do, was speaking to the public and the media. It didn't hurt that he looked like he was straight from central casting, especially when he was wearing

Opposite: The Flume—before, during and after construction

The old tunnel intake, before it was replaced

his hard hat. Everyone was used to seeing him out on the lake in his boat, talking to people, removing milfoil, addressing other issues, helping out and making friends. The media and Lake Tapps community already loved him, and with his plain spoken, credible manner Joe was just what Cascade needed right now to meet the public.

A public meeting was held in June 2014 to share with the Lake Tapps community the upcoming work projects and the impact to them. The message was big, but simple. The reservoir would be drawn down immediately after Labor Day 2014 and it would be brought down significantly to allow for 16 major repair, enhanced or rebuilding projects as well as have the reservoir down so far it would allow crews to walk inside the pipes and complete assessments. Cascade knew most of what needed to be done, but wanted to be sure everything that needed to be fixed could be identified and repaired during this one major drawdown.

The community came to the meeting as it always did. Cascade announced its plan to begin the project in mid-2104, draw the reservoir down after Labor Day and complete all the projects by mid-March 2015. To do this work, Cascade would have to draw the reservoir down from

The Barrier Structure apron, before and after, to better save the fish

the recreational level of 541.5 feet elevation to around 500 feet. Residents listened and were pleased there would only be a one-time drawdown. They were also happy there was a plan to keep the public informed every step of the way. A dedicated webpage with status information was posted and updated regularly, Facebook and Twitter were also used and postcards and mailings were sent. Plus, ads were taken out in the Bonney Lake newspapers. Once again, effective and proactive communication from Cascade made for smoother sailing.

Keeping the community informed with mailings

Opposite: Top left: flow tubes; Top right: replaced flow tubes; Middle left: relief valve; Middle right: dike three; Bottom right: old headgates; Bottom left: new headgates

The design, permitting, bidding and construction efforts involved almost all parts of the 100-plus year old system. It included the following replacements, improvements and enhancements:

- Fish screen repairs;
- Concrete flume replacement;
- Lead paint cleanup in the powerhouse;
- Fish screen replacement;
- Valve repairs;
- Improvements at the headworks;
- Dike 3 seepage mitigation and seismic remediation construction;
- Dike instrumentation (piezometers);
- Barrier structure apron repair and improvements begun;
- Reservoir debris removal;
- Improvements at the tunnel intake;
- Fixes to the headworks;
- River Road Bridge repair, and much more.

Contrary to many large scale projects where work is scheduled over time, "the [Lake Tapps] projects were all done on time," explained Chuck

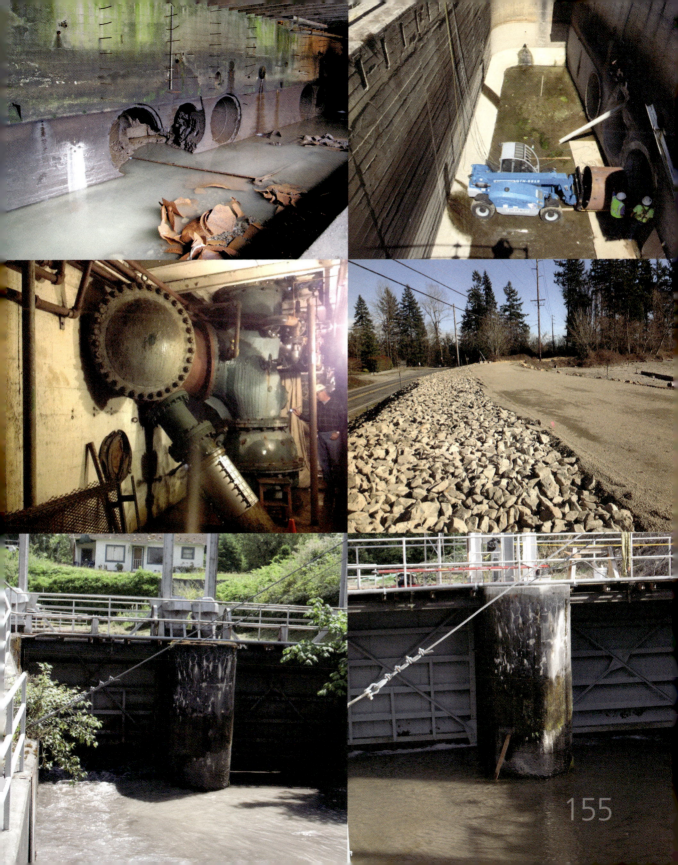

> "We were able to get the work done, respond to changes and new issues, and complete the work before our deadline. This is nothing short of phenomenal. Joe, Veolia, the Tribes, and the construction firms did a tremendous job."

Clarke. "We were able to get the work done, respond to changes and new issues, and complete the work before our deadline. This is nothing short of phenomenal. Joe, Veolia, the Tribes, and the construction firms did a tremendous job."

Things were going well. All that was left was to wait for the water. Traditionally, water that fills Lake Tapps comes from the runoff from the Emmons Glacier on Mount Rainer into the White River, as well as rain. This water is then diverted from the White River through the flume into the reservoir. In March, with the projects all completed on time, rain began flowing back into the reservoir and the fill began. And then it stopped. The usual northwest spring rain just stopped.

Precipitation in late March, April, May and June 2015 fell to about 50 percent of historic low flows. July was the hottest month on record. There was no snowpack to melt and therefore no runoff. Still, Cascade data and modeling had shown that with even the lowest historic flows it could fill the reservoir by Memorial Day. But as that holiday got closer it was clear that there was no water and fill was highly unlikely. Then in April, Washington Gov. Jay Inslee declared a drought in Eastern Washington and later extended it to the west side of the state including East Pierce County, where the reservoir was. In May, Cascade announced it would not be able to fully fill the reservoir by Memorial Day.

With only a trickle of water coming into the reservoir, most people understood and only wanted to know what the projections were. Some had events they had planned for the summer and wanted to

Lake Tapps' Leon Stucki confers with Cascade's Joe Mickelson and Chuck Clarke at the Barrier Structure

Drawdown of the reservoir 2015
(Photo by Janice Thomas)

know if they should change them. However, there were some people who were just angry and a handful who were abusive. It was a frustrating turn of events to have such great public support and to finish ahead of schedule only to have nature have the last word. It was small comfort that, under signed agreements, Cascade was legally allowed to have the reservoir drawn down for such contingencies. Neither the neighbors nor Cascade were satisfied.

"We worked with local mayors who had parks on the lake, fish and wildlife, as well as the fire and rescue and law enforcement crews," Mickelson recounts. "We wanted everyone to know what was happening. At this point, there were still a lot of places that could not yet access the lake and most chose not yet to open parks or boat launches."

In addition, there were woody debris and logs from the bottom of the reservoir that had floated up to the surface and were floating by docks. Cascade put receptacles for these at the Pierce County Park, Allan Yorke Park and the Tapps Island boat launches. With that done, and with water continuing to very slowly fill the reservoir, Cascade went ahead and opened the lake to all recreation before Fourth of July 2015.

"Cascade was working hard to refill Lake Tapps. This opportunity allowed us to align the Corps' mission of flood control and a repair which will protect fish in the river with our ability to take water for refill," said Clarke. *"We gained significantly more water going into the reservoir than we would have had without this project."*

ANOTHER PLAN FOR WATER

During most of the Lake Tapps improvement project, the US Army Corps of Engineers also had a project to protect endangered fish in the White River. The Corps utilizes Cascade's Buckley barrier structure as a component of its system to transport endangered salmon above Mud Mountain Dam. The Corps was required under federal mandate by the National Marine Fisheries Service's recent biological opinion to repair the downstream apron on the barrier structure so as not to harm or kill fish.

While the project technically began in early 2014, the effort was actually realized in April and May of 2015. Chuck Clarke immediately saw an opportunity for Cascade to put additional water into the refill.

To make the apron repair, the Corps had to reduce instream flows and is authorized to do so in order to meet the federal requirement under the Endangered Species Act. This instream flow reduction is specific to the apron repair only. Cascade is not authorized to hold water back or change instream flows.

Cascade and the Corps worked together under a cooperative agreement to maintain the Buckley barrier structure. The apron was currently in such poor condition that it not only jeopardized fish but threatened the entire barrier structure.

During the initial phase of the project, set for the first week of June, the Corps managed water flow for the safety of work crews in the river by holding water above Mud Mountain Dam. The stored water was, upon completion of the work, released into the river and Clarke arranged for Cascade to take the significant portion of water in excess of instream flows to supplement the reservoir refill.

Cascade staff watching project progress at the Barrier Structure

"Cascade was working hard to refill Lake Tapps. This opportunity allowed us to align the Corps' mission of flood control and a repair which will protect fish in the river with our ability to take water for refill," said Clarke. "We gained significantly more water going into the reservoir than we would have had without this project."

The additional water was projected to raise the reservoir considerably by the middle of June. A second phase of the Corps' project occurred near the end of June, allowing Cascade to add more water. With a third phase in late July/early August, even more would be added. When the Corps' project was completed, Lake Tapps finally reached recreational levels on Aug. 8.

"Had Cascade been a different kind of operation, like a larger bureaucracy, there is no way we could have done what we did from inception, planning, design and permitting of this project in 2013 to

"Had Cascade been a different kind of operation, like a larger bureaucracy, there is no way we could have done what we did from inception, planning, design and permitting of this project in 2013 to construction and completion 18 months later. Simply not possible," said Clarke. "What Joe and Veolia and other contractors did was nothing short of miraculous. Had this lake failed, or any of its systems failed—which was very likely—this reservoir would have been down for two years. Homeowners would have hated that even more." Instead, Lake Tapps remained full.

Opposite: Magnificent Lake Tapps (Photo by Janice Thomas)

construction and completion 18 months later. Simply not possible," said Clarke. "What Joe and Veolia and other contractors did was nothing short of miraculous. Had this lake failed, or any of its systems failed—which was very likely—this reservoir would have been down for two years. Homeowners would have hated that even more." Instead, Lake Tapps remained full.

Cascade operates Lake Tapps for recreation, municipal drinking water supply and to protect instream flows for fish. Water for municipal purposes will not likely be needed from Lake Tapps for years to come. But Cascade has worked hard to get it in the best shape it can be, healthy, mechanically sound and functioning reliably, making Lake Tapps a very viable reservoir.

"What the Cascade folks have done is protect our lake, our homes and our lifestyle," said Ralph Mason. "They need it for water supply but they've been very good about making sure it's good for us as well."

Mickelson says the relationship Cascade has built with the homeowners is based on trust, good communication and honesty. "They know we really care."

13.
ADOLESCENCE, AND HEADING INTO ADULTHOOD

As a result of owning Lake Tapps, Cascade had its water source. But, with the renegotiated contracts with Tacoma and Seattle, the need to build Lake Tapps had greatly diminished. The region had sufficient water for the future through collaboration and partnerships.

In 2014, Cascade would turn 15 years old and what a history it had achieved in its short life. Its members continued to be very involved. Partners in water and partners around Lake Tapps and even former adversaries were working together. Critical legislation had been passed. Cascade was able to operate on a lean, efficient and nimble basis.

Cascade had successfully learned there was a need to gather people together frequently to share information and work toward common goals. And what better way to keep the ball rolling than through a celebration—a birthday party—for Cascade's 15th anniversary.

But this celebration needed to be more than just the symbolic "cake ceremony" Cascade had adopted from the Lake Tapps Task Force. The event needed to be one of bringing the region together, and of giving back to the water community. For the first time in recent memory, all water providers were getting along. All municipalities were getting along. Staffs from all agencies worked together, creating and sharing tremendous amounts data and information about the future.

Opposite: Cascade Water Alliance celebrates 15 years of ensuring safe, clean and reliable water to its members

PRACTICING MORE COLLABORATION

At this time, Chuck Clarke, along with Ray Hoffman, director of Seattle Public Utilities, Jim Miller, engineering superintendent, City of Everett, and Linda McCrea, superintendent of Tacoma Water, were leading the Central Puget Sound Water Supply Forum, a cooperative effort of representatives of public water systems that addresses current and future water supply issues facing the Central Puget Sound region. The Forum was in the beginning stages of planning for regional resiliency of water supply. It made perfect sense to include the Forum in Cascade's 15th Anniversary celebration.

So, Clarke and Cascade board members decided to turn its 15th anniversary event into a day of workshops informing others of the issues Cascade and members of the Forum were exploring surrounding the future of the region's water supply. The event would include appearances by experts who could share with the area's water providers what was going on with water supply across the country—from the very dry southwest, and the lessons learned there, to the very real dangers to utilities of earthquakes, drought, climate change and water quality issues.

It became an opportunity to educate key decision makers and elected officials about what happens when you don't plan or are not prepared for the future. The birthday party became a showcase for Cascade and fellow Forum members to share with smaller providers what they were doing and invite them to become a part of it. And it would show all interested parties that the spirit of cooperation Cascade and others had fostered through the two legislative outreach efforts and this inclusive celebration was the tone the region could take moving forward.

SETTING THE STAGE

The event was held May 15, 2014 at Bellevue's Meydenbauer Center. An outstanding series of speakers and highly anticipated workshops had been set up. While attendance of about 150 had been planned for, registration swelled to double, with participants keenly interested in what they could learn from the gathered experts and the burgeoning regional effort that was getting underway.

Cascade invited nationally recognized utility leader planner Pat Mulroy as the keynote breakfast speaker. Pat is the retired general manager of the Southern Nevada Water Authority and had been at the helm of regional water crises that pulled the region together to solve critical water shortages. It wasn't easy, she said, but they had faced a crisis and had no choice but to act. But a region that understands and plans for crises and the need for forged solutions can make a difference. Her message for attendees as she left them spoke from her experiences: Are your water agencies of the 21st Century able to adapt?

Clarke also called up his fellow major utility directors, Ray Hoffman, Linda McCrae and Jim Miller to step forward. Like Mulroy, these leaders had seen what had occurred elsewhere in the country and individually decided their large utility could not put off planning for the future. Each utility demonstrated several areas for which they had prepared. Seattle had begun resiliency planning with particular attention to climate change and its potential impacts. Tacoma had redundant pipelines feeding its city and extensive interties with other utilities as well as resiliency in source, climate change and infrastructure with a plan for next steps. Everett had examined reliability and resiliency projects, looked at the cost benefit ratio and prioritized the projects. They dealt with natural hazards, other threats to a system and determined earthquakes had the potential greatest effect and that upgrades were essential. The

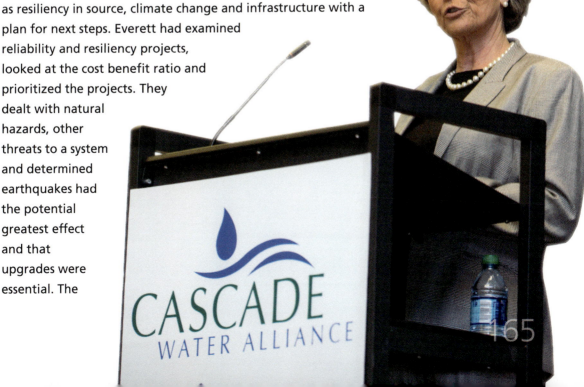

Patricia Mulroy, retired general manager of the Southern Nevada Water Authority, addresses the attendees

"None of us," Clarke concluded, "Can do this alone."

Jim Miller, engineering superintendent, City of Everett, Linda McCrea, superintendent of Tacoma Water, Ray Hoffman, director of Seattle Public Utilities and Chuck Clarke, CEO of Cascade Water Alliance, share their thoughts with attendees

conclusion they reached separately and together as the Forum, was that it made sense to plan together as a region. "None of us," Clarke concluded, "Can do this alone."

The 300 participants clearly saw the need for that as well. They funneled into workshops that focused on recognizing and preparing for water supply risks from various earthquake scenarios to climate change. Another panel discussed resilience through sustainable revenues, such as credit worthiness, financial revenue trends and sustainability, emergency financial response/drought rates and responding to market demand erosion.

As the workshops ended, somber and thoughtful attendees returned to Meydenbauer's main dining room where participants were riveted throughout a lively presentation by Will Stelle, the administrator of National Marine Fisheries Services of NOAA's Northwest Division. Stelle had been a fixture in water issues of the Northwest for two decades. His position at NMFS showed him first hand the impacts of the drought in California—the angst, the challenges and critical issues—and the lessons the Northwest could learn about resiliency from that experience.

WORDS OF WISDOM AND PARTNERSHIP

Cascade's Chair John Marchione concluded the day's events. He addressed the crowd, saying, "Today, we have all heard what is facing other parts of the country. We are all in this room together and I think you'll agree the warning is clear. We need to work together to address the issue of resiliency today or we face what the Southwest and California are facing. As Cascade celebrates its 15th anniversary we wanted to thank our partners—the City of Seattle, Tacoma Water, Everett Water—the four cities around Lake Tapps, the Puyallup and Muckleshoot Tribes and our Lake Tapps Community. We couldn't have been as successful as we have been without them.

"But I think the message of regional partnerships goes beyond that. What we heard today is we need to put our collective efforts together as we plan for what is needed in our region—and how we can get there. What I learned today is that we have threats and risks facing us. We've

> "Cascade's first board members had a vision. They wanted a voice and a vote in their destiny—and that meant having water for their own growth and economic development. I'm a fifth generation Washingtonian. I want my kids and theirs to have what we have. And to do that, we have to address tomorrow together."

seen the results of how other regions address their challenges. We'd done a tremendous amount of work separately and together. But we need to build on these efforts.

"Cascade's first board members had a vision. They wanted a voice and a vote in their destiny—and that meant having water for their own growth and economic development. I'm a fifth generation Washingtonian. I want my kids and theirs to have what we have. And to do that, we have to address tomorrow together."

Jim Haggerton, Tukwila mayor, was on Cascade's board for 15 years, the last two as vice chair. He asked, "What does everything we've heard here today mean for the region? I have served in many capacities throughout the region, but I have never seen a more focused, positive and visionary effort. Individually we are all investing in our own future with planning and investments.

Cascade Vice Chair Jim Haggerton, Mayor of Tukwila, greets guests.

"But sitting here is a network of water suppliers that sees the importance of putting into practice a truly regional planning effort to be ready for tomorrow. At today's workshops, they called it resilience. What does that mean? It means working together to have a plan. If you have an emergency, you will have water. If you have a need, you will have water. And Cascade and the region have Lake Tapps as a future water supply source should we ever need it."

Lloyd Warren reflected that, "Cascade has been able to set precedents in water supply policy. It also allows Cascade to be an important part of the "Big Four" water supplier."

Chuck Clarke added, "Water planning takes decades. Today we're celebrating successes. We have been successful in our adolescence. Our partnerships mean we can provide the lowest cost of service delivery to everyone involved. But what's even more exciting is the regional partnerships and collaboration that's being done today for the future.

"Today we are doing our job as a region. Together we are providing for the region's future environment, water supply, recreation and culture. I'm proud to be part of Cascade on its 15th birthday but even more excited to be part of what our region seems poised and ready to do to be ready for tomorrow."

It was a stellar celebration indeed. The crowd of 300 influential decision makers and water supply planners left the room engaged and energized. Evaluations from the event overwhelmingly indicated utilities and key decision makers wanted more information, workshops and getting ahead of the curve by acting now.

FIFTEEN YEARS OF WATER AND WORK

The need for and creation of Cascade had ripped apart the water community decades before in the Puget Sound region. Time, change of players, political will, Cascade's purchase of Lake Tapps and a softening water demand (as a result of wiser water use), eventually brought the region together again to plan for the future. Fred Butler, Issaquah mayor and Cascade board chair, describes Cascade as a lean, nimble water leader that sits at the table with the other water powers in the region. Its governance model is efficient and effective. Its collaborative efforts have built credibility and its leaders trust.

But, was this how those who began Cascade envisioned its future and impact? Jon Ault, a Skyway Water and

Lloyd Warren honors the Puyallup Indian Tribe (John Bell) and Muckleshoot Tribe of Indians representatives (Todd La Clair) for their partnership. (Elaine: photo/clip is lo-res for now...)

Cascade's longest serving board member, Jon Ault, president of the Skyway Water and Sewer District commission

Sewer District commissioner for 18 years, and with Cascade since its inception, remembered, "Our vision was to have a voice and be a part of a community so we didn't have to go it alone. Most folks don't care where the water comes from—they just want it on when they need it. It's been interesting to be a part of the collective thinking for the future and that we actually got there. Skyway was proud to be one of the founding partners to sign the Cascade agreement. I'm proud of that and what we've become."

Cascade has become an effective part of the region, said John Marchione, Redmond mayor and chair of Cascade as it turned 15. "It's a vital part of keeping this area viable. For that to continue, we have to have a reliable source of clean water for all of us to use."

Marchione's mother, Doreen, is also on the Cascade board representing Kirkland. She, too, was once Redmond's mayor and commented that "What makes for success is having leaders you trust to move issues forward. Lots of work goes on behind the scenes, and the winners are our customers. There was a leadership vacuum and we filled it, working together despite lots of other differences."

Cascade is respected regionally, in the state and even nationally as a model of how municipalities can work together to get important decisions made through regional cooperation and problem solving. And, from the Lake Tapps community perspective, Kirk Shuler added that he and his neighbors were very worried about the future of the reservoir. But now "Cascade has become a very good partner and gone beyond our expectations. They've been a good model. A resource that wasn't possible any other way. A win-win."

Walt Canter, who has been on the water scene since 1969, sees Cascade's impact from a longer lens. "I never had good relations with the cities and counties. I didn't buy into Cascade or its need, but others did and they kept probing and trying things. They had a group with common objectives and developed it and modified it over time to make it work. Vision, plan and do. Make it happen. They used all their talents and skills and discipline in a joint effort. Some of us were opposed, but when different backgrounds and different needs come together for a critical resource like the good dedicated conscientious people in water—well, it works."

As to the success of Cascade, former Bellevue Mayor and Cascade Board member Don Davidson said it's a legacy of which he's very proud. "It's all about synergy. Set a goal and get on it and focus on a goal. You can get there. And more importantly, like Cascade and like the Forum work, it's a sustainable legacy that goes beyond who's at the table."

Former Seattle Mayor Norm Rice reflected that, "There should be a regional government and powers vested into one system. We need to broker collaboration to help us become a true region. Looking back, I might have been more aggressive to get a better governance model over water and other critical services. We also need leaders who are less partisan, forward thinking people with a sense of region and where it's going," Rice said.

He added, "Water today is close to coming full circle. We no longer have urban and suburban. We are all urban and we need to talk together about the impacts on all the region even if it takes a long time to get there. Money makes us rethink things. Separate systems are expensive and need to be connected by governance. My background is built around a federated government, collaboration and no specific constituency. You need to understand all the issues and impacts. We need leaders and leadership like we have right now to create consensus. Cascade's work and the others all coming together have helped us define critical regional issues and they are asking the right questions—what's best for our region. Bring everyone together and get the right people at the table. Create a plan and execute. Basic. Simple. But it works."

Lloyd Warren, largely credited with the staff work that created

John Marchione, Cascade, Will Stelle, NOAA and Linda McCrea, Tacoma Water

> We need leaders and leadership like we have right now to create consensus. Cascade's work and the others all coming together have helped us define critical regional issues and they are asking the right questions—what's best for our region. Bring everyone together and get the right people at the table. Create a plan and execute. Basic. Simple. But it works."

Cascade, has served as its chair and is still on the board. An integral part of Cascade at every step of its existence, he summed it up saying, "We got our voice and our vote. And we got water supply with Lake Tapps. Cascade made a great decision to buy the lake but it also brought a change in perspective. Lake Tapps' future water supply allowed us to be at the table to work with other providers. Now Cascade is part of the regional resiliency planning. That would not have been possible before, so in many ways it's very important investment for Cascade and possibly the region in the future. Cascade is still the agency in the region dealing with potential for meeting new regional demands, and, as such, has driven the marketplace. This has not only allowed Cascade to be an important part of the big four water suppliers (Cascade with Seattle, Tacoma and Everett) it has also allowed us to set precedents in water supply policy."

Hugh Spitzer, the Seattle attorney who has been so involved in municipal law, added, "Today, Cascade is the connective tissue, with its service areas running north to south to others [Seattle, Tacoma and Everett] that run east to west. It rebalanced the region regarding water and will help set the course for the future."

And unlike other regional problems that seem to be always behind the times and catching up, former Cascade board member, Mary Alyce Burleigh of Kirkland, said "Cascade has shown how you can be proactive and get to a solution before it becomes a problem. Regional. That was truly our vision and it's exceeded that."

Grant Degginger said Cascade is what every official strives for—"to leave our home in a better position than when we took charge." Cascade exemplifies that. "We made decisions over the last decades to ensure the future of tomorrow."

Thirty years ago, when Jim Miller (now engineering superintendent for the City of Everett) left Seattle to go to work in to Federal Way, he told people he expected a time when he'd see Everett, Seattle and Tacoma connected and that Federal Way would be seeing some of that water. Maybe he wasn't too far off.

Since that day, members of the Water Supply Forum, which represents Cascade, Tacoma, Seattle and Everett and most, of the water systems in the three-county area and most of the population served and water supplied have come together in an unprecedented planning effort to help the central Puget Sound region better prepare for the impacts of significant system stresses and enhance water supply system resiliency.

In total, these utilities serve approximately 2.3 million people over 1,200 square miles. The region served includes approximately 60 cities/water districts, a major metropolitan area, three bustling ports, and world-class businesses that have international headquarters or major

Jim Miller, engineering superintendent for Everett, and Ray Hoffman, director of Seattle Public Utilities, share their thoughts on the future of water and how the region is addressing that future together

The story of Cascade Water Alliance is far from over. But 15 years into its history it's looking forward to the future and what can be seen looks amazing.

Beyond a voice… there is now a vision.

operations in the Seattle area including Weyerhaeuser, Starbucks, Amazon, Microsoft, and Boeing.

Without crises or mandated efforts, the Forum member utilities have worked across jurisdictional boundaries and brought together staff with expertise in engineering, planning and the sciences to evaluate the water supply system risks facing the central Puget Sound region and identify opportunities to improve the region's resiliency to these risks and recommendations as to how to best address them for the public health and safety of the region.

Ray Hoffman, SPU Director, says, "Enough time has passed. We in Seattle have a good working model, and now all the other water providers in the regional have more similarities than differences. The Forum work is some of the most important work we've done and we expect a report to the water utilities and community at large in 2016. The best thing we can all do for our customers is for us to talk to other providers and know what's going on and be able to assist others in the region. We cannot afford to play ostrich any more regarding things like drought, earthquakes, climate change and water quality conditions. We are all in one big boat. We should all take a moment to acknowledge that the region is blessed with the highest quality and best protected water supply in the country. We should all realize that. And we are the stewards of that supply."

The story of Cascade Water Alliance is far from over. But 15 years into its history it's looking forward to the future and what can be seen looks amazing.

Beyond a voice… there is now a vision.

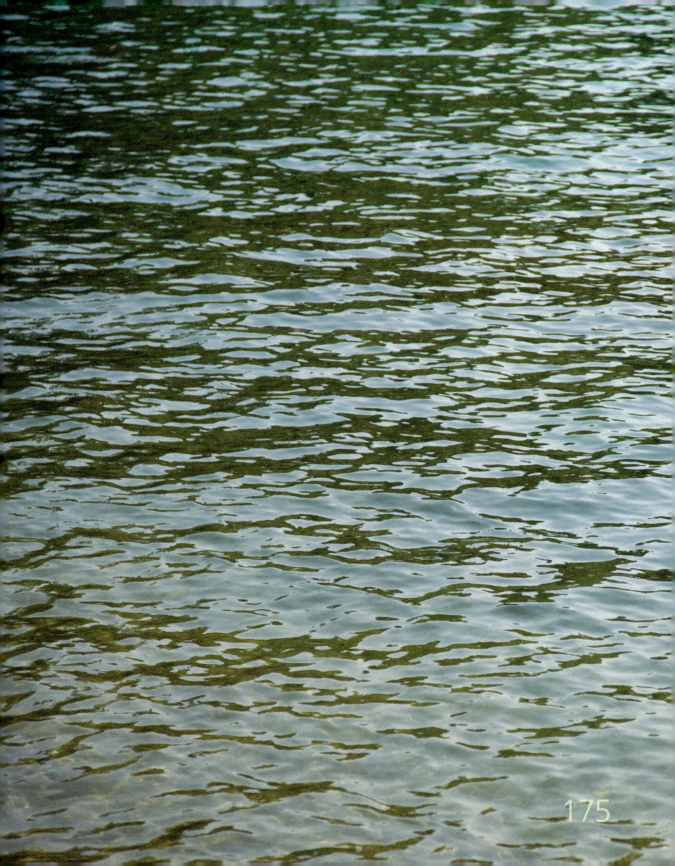

APPENDICES

APPENDIX A
CASCADE KEY DOCUMENTS

The following information can be found on Cascade's web site at www.cascadewater.org

Document	Executed
1954 Deed	6.22.1954
Quitclaim Deed from Lake Tapps Development Company to Puget Sound Power and Light	12.3.1958
Cascade Articles of Incorporation	4.27.1999
Cascade By Laws	5.19.1999
Cascade Interlocal Contracts	10.5.1999
Seattle Public Utilities-Cascade 50 Year Declining Block Water Supply Agreement	12.15.2003
Transmission and Supply Plan (TSP) 2004	9.29.2005
Tacoma-Cascade agreement for Sale of Water	10.13.2006
PSE-Cascade term sheet	
Lake Tapps Purchase Agreement	4.23.2008
White River Management Agreement (Tribes)	8.6.2008
Amended Block Water Supply Agreement with Seattle	12.17.2008
2009 Agreement with Lake Tapps Homeowners	5.12.2009
Four Cities Agreement—Water Resources Agreement	2.5.2010
Lake Tapps Water Rights	9.15.2010
Water Rights Permits	12.10.2010

Document	Executed
Transmission and Supply Plan 2012	7.2012
Joint Municipal Utilities Services Authorization Recorded	7.24.2012
Cascade-Tacoma Amended Sale of Wholesale Water	12.31.2012
Cascade-Seattle 2nd Amended Declining Water Supply Agreement	7.15.2013
TSP Update to Departments of Ecology and Health	8.02.2013
Cascade Lake Tapps Trust Water Right Agreement	12.03.2014
Trust Water Right	01.08.2015

APPENDIX B
CASCADE CHRONOLOGY

1889 Washington becomes the 42nd state to enter the Union. Without contracts or local representation Seattle provides water to local region.

1911 Puget Sound Energy's White River Project begins to generate power

1982 Seattle enters into 30-year agreement with 27 regional water purveyors

1991 Formation of Tri-Caucus (Seattle, Suburban Cities Association and King County Water Alliance)

1995 Planning for development of new water supply sources for future begins by Tri Caucus participants

1996 An Interim Water Group forms to create a new water service provider entity

1997 Multi utility agreement for developing Tacoma's Second Supply Project (Tacoma, Seattle, Kent, Lakehaven Utilities District and Covington Water)

1998 Cascade Water Alliance organization planning complete. Membership opens to agencies

1999 Cascade Water Alliance created by Bellevue, Issaquah, Kirkland, Redmond, Tukwila, Sammamish Plateau Water and Sewer, Skyway Water and Sewer and Covington Water District. (Other original members who did not continue as members include Duvall, Mercer Island and Woodinville Water District.)

2001 Cascade and Puget Sound Energy enter into agreement to jointly pursue water rights for Lake Tapps

Seattle offers water purveyors new 60-year full or partial requirements contracts.

2003	Cascade signs declining block contract with Seattle for water
2004	PSE halts all power production on White River Project and agrees with Lake Tapps community to try to save recreation at the lake
	Cascade adopts initial Transmission and Supply Plan (TSP)
2005	Cascade and PSE execute term sheet related to Cascade acquisition of Lake Tapps
	Seattle drops out of participation in Tacoma Second Supply Project
	Cascade signs Tacoma Wholesale Water agreement
2008	Cascade signs agreement with Puyallup Tribe of Indians and Muckleshoot Indian Tribe regarding in-stream flows on the White River (White River Management Agreement)
	Cascade and Seattle amend declining block contract for additional water supply
2009	Cascade purchases Lake Tapps from PSE
	Cascade and the Lake Tapps community sign agreement regarding maintenance of lake levels (Lake Tapps Homeowners Agreement)
2010	Cascade issues environmental impact statement; DOE issues water rights
	Cascade and the cities of Auburn, Bonney Lake, Buckley and Sumner sign Lake Tapps Area Water Resource Agreement regarding the four cities' future water use
2012	Cascade becomes the first municipal corporation under the Joint Municipal Utilities Services Act
	2012 TSP contains plan for 50 plus year water supply
2053	Expiration of Cascade Supply Agreement with Seattle

APPENDIX C
CASCADE WATER ALLIANCE BOARD MEMBERS AND ALTERNATES

Year	City/Utility	Board Member	Board Position	Alternate Board Member
1999	Bellevue	Chuck Mosher	Chair	NA
	Woodinville Water District	Maureen Jewitt	Vice Chair	Gail Harrell, Gwenn Maxfield
	Mercer Island	Alan Merkel	Secretary/Treasurer	El Jahnke
	Covington WD	Lys Hornsby	Board Member	NA
	Bryn Mawr Lakeridge WSD	Albert Blanchard	Board Member	John Ault
	Duvall	Mark Cole	Board Member	Pat Fullmer
	Issaquah	Bill Conley	Board Member	Ava Frisinger
	Kirkland	Sants Contreras	Board Member	Nona Ganz
	Redmond	Rosemarie Ives	Board Member	Sharon Dorning
	Sammamish Plateau WSD	Steve Stevlingson	Board Member	Robert George
	Tukwila	Jim Haggerton	Board Member	Steve Mullet
2000	Bryn Mawr Lakeridge WSD	Albert Blanchard	Chair	John Ault
	Woodinville Water District	Maureen Jewitt	Vice Chair	Gail Harrell, Gwenn Maxfield
	Mercer Island	Alan Merkel	Secretary/Treasure	El Jahnke
	Bellevue	Chuck Mosher	Board Member	NA
	Covington WD	Lys Hornsby	Board Member	NA

Year	City/Utility	Board Member	Board Position	Alternate Board Member
2000	Duvall	Mark Cole	Board Member	Pat Fullmer
	Issaquah	Bill Conley	Board Member	Ava Frisinger
	Kirkland	Sants Contreras	Board Member	Nona Ganz
	Redmond	Rosemarie Ives	Board Member	Sharon Dorning
	Sammamish Plateau WSD	Steve Stevlingson	Board Member	Robert George
	Tukwila	Jim Haggerton	Board Member	Steve Mullet, Pam Carter
2001	Bryn Mawr Lakeridge WSD	Albert Blanchard	Chair	John Ault
	Woodinville Water District	Maureen Jewitt	Vice Chair	Gail Harrell, Gwenn Maxfield
	Mercer Island	Alan Merkel	Secretary/Treasurer	El Jahnke
	Covington	Lys Hornsby	Board Member	NA
	Bellevue	Grant Degginger	Board Member	Don Davidson
	Duvall	Mark Cole	Board Member	Pat Fullmer
	Issaquah	Joe Forkner	Board Member	Bill Conley
	Kirkland	Sants Contreras	Board Member	Nona Ganz
	Redmond	Rosemarie Ives	Board Member	Sharon Dorning
	Sammamish Plateau WSD	Steve Stevlingson	Board Member	Robert George
	Tukwila	Jim Haggerton	Board Member	Steve Mullet, Pam Carter
2002	Bellevue	Grant Degginger	Chair	Don Davidson
	Woodinville Water District	Maureen Jewitt	Vice Chair	Gwen Maxfield
	Skyway WSD	Al Blanchard	Secretary/Treasurer	John Ault
	Mercer Island	Dan Grausz	Board Member	El Jahnke
	Covington WD	Lys Hornsby	Board Member	NA
	Issaquah	Joe Forkner	Board Member	Bill Conley
	Kirkland	Sants Contreras	Board Member	Mary-Alyce Burleigh
	Redmond	Rosemarie Ives	Board Member	Sharon Dorning

Year	City/Utility	Board Member	Board Position	Alternate Board Member
2002	Sammamish Plateau WSD	Stanley Stone	Board Member	Steve Stevlingson
	Tukwila	Jim Haggerton	Vice Chair	Steve Mullet, Pam Carter
2003	Bellevue	Grant Degginger	Chair	Don Davidson
	Tukwila	Jim Haggerton	Vice Chair	Steve Mullet, Pam Carter
	Skyway WSD	Albert Blanchard	Secretary/Treasurer	John Ault
	Mercer Island	Dan Grausz	Board Member	El Jahnke
	Covington WD	Lys Hornsby	Board Member	NA
	Issaquah	Joe Forkner	Board Member	Bill Conley
	Kirkland	Mary-Alyce Burleigh	Board Member	Sants Contreras
	Redmond	Rosemarie Ives	Board Member	Sharon Dorning
	Sammamish Plateau WSD	Stanley Stone	Board Member	Steve Stevlingson
2004	Bellevue	Grant Degginger	Chair	Don Davidson
	Sammamish Plateau WSD	Stanley Stone	Vice Chair	Steve Stevlingson
	Tukwila	Jim Haggerton	Secretary/Treasurer	Steve Mullet, Pam Carter
	Skyway WSD	John Ault	Board Member	NA
	Mercer Island	Dan Grausz	Board Member	El Jahnke
	Covington WD	Lys Hornsby	Board Member	NA
	Issaquah	Joe Forkner	Board Member	Bill Conley
	Kirkland	Mary-Alyce Burleigh	Board Member	Jim Lauinger
	Redmond	John Marchione	Board Member	Rosemarie Ives
2005	Bellevue	Grant Degginger	Chair	Don Davidson
	Sammamish Plateau WSD	Lloyd Warren	Vice Chair	Stanley Stone
	Tukwila	Jim Haggerton	Secretary/Treasurer	Steve Mullet, Pam Carter

Year	City/Utility	Board Member	Board Position	Alternate Board Member
2005	Skyway WSD	John Ault	Board Member	NA
	Mercer Island	Dan Grausz	Board Member	El Jahnke
	Covington WD	Lys Hornsby	Board Member	David Knight
	Issaquah	Joe Forkner	Board Member	Bill Conley
	Kirkland	Mary-Alyce Burleigh	Board Member	Jim Lauinger
	Redmond	John Marchione	Board Member	Rosemarie Ives
2006	Bellevue	Grant Degginger	Chair	Don Davidson
	Sammamish Plateau WSD	Lloyd Warren	Vice Chair	Stanley Stone
	Tukwila	Jim Haggerton	Secretary/Treasurer	Steve Mullet, Pam Carter
	Covington WD	Lys Hornsby	Board Member	David Knight
	Issaquah	David Kappler	Board Member	Nancy Davidson
	Kirkland	Mary-Alyce Burleigh	Board Member	Jim Lauinger
	Redmond	Jon Marchione	Board Member	Rosemarie Ives
	Skyway WSD	Jon Ault	Board Member	NA
2007	Bellevue	Grant Degginger	Chair	Don Davidson
	Sammamish Plateau WSD	Lloyd Warren	Vice Chair	Stanley Stone
	Tukwila	Jim Haggerton	Secretary/Treasurer	Steve Mullet
	Covington WD	David Knight	Board Member	Jeff Clark
	Issaquah	Joe Forkner	Board Member	John Rittenhouse
	Kirkland	Mary-Alyce Burleigh	Board Member	Jim Lauinger
	Redmond	Jon Marchione	Board Member	Rosemarie Ives
	Skyway WSD	Jon Ault	Board Member	Joyce Clark
2008	Sammamish Plateau WSD	Lloyd Warren	Chair	Steve Stevlingson
	Kirkland	Mary Alyce Burleigh	Vice Chair	Jim Lauinger
	Tukwila	Jim Haggerton	Secretary/Treasurer	Verna Griffin

Year	City/Utility	Board Member	Board Position	Alternate Board Member
2008	Bellevue	Grant Degginger	Board Member	Don Davidson
	Redmond	John Marchione	Board Member	Nancy McCormick
	Skyway WSD	Jon Ault	Board Member	Joyce Clark
	Covington Water District	David Knight	Board Member	Jeff Clark
	Issaquah	David Kappler	Board Member	John Traeger
2009	Sammamish Plateau WSD	Lloyd Warren	Chair	Robert Brady
	Kirkland	Mary Alyce Burleigh	Vice Chair	Jim Lauinger
	Tukwila	Jim Haggerton	Secretary/Treasurer	Verna Griffin
	Issaquah	David Kappler	Board Member	John Traeger
	Bellevue	Grant Degginger	Board Member	Don Davidson
	Redmond	John Marchione	Board Member	Nancy McCormick
	Covington Water District	David Knight	Board Member	Jeff Clark
	Skyway WSD	Jon Ault	Board Member	Joyce Clark
2010	Sammamish Plateau WSD	Lloyd Warren	Chair	Robert Brady
	Redmond	John Marchione	Vice Chair	Hank Margeson
	Tukwila	Jim Haggerton	Secretary/Treasurer	Verna Griffin
	Bellevue	Grant Degginger	Board Member	Don Davidson
	Issaquah	John Traeger	Board Member	Mark Mullet
	Kirkland	Penny Sweet	Board Member	Doreen Marchione
	Covington Water District	David Knight	Board Member	Jeff Clark
	Skyway WSD	Jon Ault	Board Member	Joyce Clark
2011	Sammamish Plateau WSD	Lloyd Warren	Chair	Robert Brady
	Redmond	John Marchione	Vice Chair	Hank Margeson

Year	City/Utility	Board Member	Board Position	Alternate Board Member
2011	Tukwila	Jim Haggerton	Secretary/Treasurer	Verna Seal
	Bellevue	Grant Degginger	Board Member	Don Davidson
	Issaquah	John Traeger	Board Member	Stacy Goodman
	Kirkland	Penny Sweet	Board Member	Doreen Marchione
	Covington WD	David Knight	Board Member	Jeff Clark
	Skyway WSD	Jon Ault	Board Member	Joyce Clark
2012	Redmond	Jon Marchione	Chair	Hank Margeson
	Covington WD	David Knight	Vice Chair	Jeff Clark
	Tukwila	Jim Haggerton	Secretary/Treasurer	Verna Seal
	Issaquah	Fred Butler	Board Member	Stacy Goodman
	Bellevue	Don Davidson	Board Member	Kevin Wallace
	Skyway WSD	Jon Ault	Board Member	C. Gary Schulz
	Kirkland	Penny Sweet	Board Member	Doreen Marchione
	Sammamish Plateau WSD	Lloyd Warren	Board Member	Robert Brady
2013	Redmond	John Marchione	Chair	Hank Margeson
	Tukwila	Jim Haggerton	Vice Chair	Verna Seal
	Issaquah	Fred Butler	Secretary/Treasurer	Stacy Goodman
	Bellevue	Don Davidson	Board Member	Kevin Wallace
	Kirkland	Penny Sweet	Board Member	Doreen Marchione
	Sammamish Plateau WSD	Lloyd Warren	Board Member	Robert Brady
	Skyway WSD	Jon Ault	Board Member	C. Gary Schulz
2014	Redmond	John Marchione	Chair	Tom Flynn
	Tukwila	Jim Haggerton	Vice Chair	Verna Seal
	Issaquah	Fred Butler	Secretary/Treasurer	Nina Milligan
	Kirkland	Penny Sweet	Board Member	Doreen Marchione

Year	City/Utility	Board Member	Board Position	Alternate Board Member
2014	Sammamish Plateau WSD	Lloyd Warren	Board Member	Bob Abbott
	Skyway WSD	Jon Ault	Board Member	C. Gary Schulz
	Bellevue	John Stokes	Board Member	Kevin Wallace
2015	Redmond	John Marchione	Chair	Tom Flynn
	Tukwila	Jim Haggerton	Vice Chair	Verna Seal
	Issaquah	Fred Butler	Secretary/Treasurer	Nina Milligan
	Kirkland	Penny Sweet	Board Member	Doreen Marchione
	Sammamish Plateau WSD	Lloyd Warren	Board Member	Mahbubul Islam
	Skyway WSD	Jon Ault	Board Member	C. Gary Schulz
	Bellevue	John Stokes	Board Member	Kevin Wallace
2016	Issaquah	Fred Butler	Chair	Mary Lou Pauley
	Bellevue	John Stokes	Vice Chair	Kevin Wallace
	Kirkland	Penny Sweet	Secretary/Treasurer	Doreeen Marchione
	Skyway WSD	Jon Ault	Board Member	C. Gary Schulz
	Redmond	John Marchione	Board Member	Angela Birney
	Sammamish Plateau Water	Lloyd Warren	Board Member	Mahbubul Islam
	Tukwila	Allen Ekberg	Board Member	Joe Duffie

ABOUT THE AUTHOR

A native Eastsider and Bellevue resident, Elaine Kraft graduated from the University of Washington in journalism and political science and got her master's degree in business/public administration from the University of Puget Sound. She began her career as a reporter for the Eastside Journal and she has since served as a communications, community relations, government, policy spokesperson and advocate for the Washington State Legislature, Weyerhaeuser, the Coors Brewing Company, the University of Washington and as communications director for King County Executive Ron Sims. She has been at Cascade Water Alliance since 2008 overseeing all external relations for and with Cascade's members to make sure the region has and will have water for the future. She also coordinates the communications and outreach for the Water Supply Forum.